Praise for *Healing the Wounds of Trauma*

"This book puts clear information about trauma in the hands of the global church. Its roots go down deep into the work of Christ on the cross and the truths of God's Word. The teachings are sound and give ample room to the importance of understanding what trauma does to human beings, the need to tell their story and to grieve. The book is a gift to the body of Jesus."

Diane Langberg, Ph.D., psychologist and author, co-chair
of Trauma Healing Advisory Council

"This is by far the best book I know of to introduce hurting, grieving, traumatized people to the Scriptures and the healing power of the cross. What's more, this book doesn't just tell you Bible truths. It creates space for real conversations about heart wounds, the purpose of lament, and the nature of spiritual flourishing in a broken world."

Philip G. Monroe, PsyD, clinical psychologist, Taylor Visiting Professor of
Counseling, Missio Seminary, co-chair of Trauma Healing Advisory Council

"I have found that it is a book I can put into the hands of church leaders. Its straightforward approach makes it easy to use. Its many biblical references touch the heart of believers who use the book. I have found that its vision and methods travel well across denominational boundaries in the Church. This is quite simply the best single little book I have seen for these purposes."

Robert J. Schreiter, C.PP.S.,
professor of theology, Catholic Theological Union

Healing the Wounds of Trauma

Facilitator Guide for Healing Groups

Stories from North America

Trauma Healing Institute

HEALING THE WOUNDS OF TRAUMA: FACILITATOR GUIDE FOR HEALING GROUPS (Stories from North America)

© 2021 American Bible Society and SIL International. All rights reserved.
Adapted and compiled from *Healing the Wounds of Trauma: How the Church Can Help*, Expanded edition © 2016 SIL International and American Bible Society; *Healing the Wounds of Trauma: How the Church Can Help*, North America edition © 2014 SIL International and American Bible Society; and *Starter Handbook for Healing Groups* © 2015, 2016 American Bible Society and SIL International.

Updated June 2021.

Special acknowledgment given to Margaret Hill, Harriet Hill, Richard Baggé, and Pat Miersma, authors of previous editions of *Healing the Wounds of Trauma: How the Church Can Help*.

This edition by Dana Ergenbright (ABS), Stacey Conard (SIM), Mary Crickmore (World Renew), Phil Monroe (ABS), Bryan Varenkamp (SIL) and Debbie Wolcott (ABS)

Trauma Healing Institute
traumahealinginstitute.org
101 North Independence Mall East
Philadelphia PA 19106

Illustrations: Ian Dale
Design: Jordan Grove, Peter Edman
Typesetting: Canadian Bible Society, Peter Edman, Rose Yancik
Cover image: Jessica Martin, © 2015. Used by permission.

ISBN 978-1-58516-799-9 / ABS Item 124979 (Paperback)
ISBN 978-1-58516-313-7 / ABS Item 125131 (ePub)

Printed in the United States of America

For use with:
Healing the Wounds of Trauma: How the Church Can Help (Stories from North America)
ISBN 9781-58516-798-2 / ABS Item 124978 (Paperback)

ISBN 978-1-58516-310-6 / ABS Item 125128 (ePub)

About *Healing the Wounds of Trauma*

In the world today, many people have experienced war, ethnic conflict, floods, car accidents, domestic abuse, or crime. Many of them have been wounded inside by these things. The Church should be helping its members who are suffering (Acts 20:28) as well as being light and salt in the world. *Healing the Wounds of Trauma: Facilitator Guide for Healing Groups* is intended to help people recover from trauma and loss. It is particularly focused on helping the local church respond to hurting people in a way that is helpful, rather than harmful. Each lesson presents what the Bible and mental health best practices teach about how to heal from trauma.

This facilitator guide contains:
- the *Healing the Wounds of Trauma* content that is in the participant book
- facilitator prompts (in italics, marked by the letter "F") which explain how to lead the sessions
- timetables, objectives, and preparation needed for each lesson
- resources for leading healing groups (see "Preparing to lead your own healing group")

This book is to be used by a certified trauma healing facilitator. To be trained in using this book, go to traumahealinginstitute.org/events.

Contents

If you have been using a previous edition of the Classic trauma healing facilitator handbook, please see the THI facilitator website for a list of updates in this edition (2021 revision updates).

Welcome

Before you begin:

- Carefully review the section "Organizing a healing group" in the back of this guide. It contains instructions on how to use this guide in managing discussions with different sizes of groups, arranging the space, managing the time, and other important principles that will help you as you facilitate your group.
- Select a "get to know one another" activity.
- Get name tags.

In this lesson we will:

- Share our name and something about ourselves with the group.
- Discuss our hopes for the group.
- Decide how we want to treat each other in the group.

Section 1: About each other	5 min
Section 2: About our group	15 min
Total time	**20 minutes**

1. About each other

(5 min) Large group. Have everyone introduce themselves and tell the name they want to be called. Give out name tags, if appropriate.

Do a simple, fun activity that helps participants get to know one another (for example, favorite food, favorite animal, happiest memory). Some people may feel unsafe sharing personal information, so be careful what you ask.

If this is an equipping session or your healing group is large, do this exercise in small groups (that is, table groups).

2. About our group

(5 min) Large group. Express the content below in your own words. If this introduction is not needed for your context, feel free to leave it out.

Some experiences in life are very painful. They can cause deep suffering that lasts a long time. This is what we call "trauma." Trauma is a deep wound of the heart and mind that takes a long time to heal. It hurts every part of our lives: how we relate to others, how our body feels, what we think about, and how much we can trust God. It can make us feel separated from God and others. We may no longer feel like the same person as before.

But God is with everyone who suffers. God knows our pain and helps us heal. So we have hope.

In this group, we will begin to heal together. We will cover at least six topics:

- If God loves us, why do we suffer?
- What is a wound of the heart?
- What can help our heart wounds heal?
- What happens when someone is grieving?
- Bringing our pain to Jesus
- How can we forgive others?

Learning what the Bible says about these topics may help us experience God's nearness and love for us. As we learn to talk about our pain and listen to the pain of others, we will discover that we are not alone.

In this group, we will be talking about our feelings and things that have happened to us. You may share as much or as little as you wish. You may feel difficult emotions at times—perhaps anger, sadness, anxiety, irritability, or tenseness. This is normal. It is part of the healing process.

This is a participatory program, not a seminar or a class. It is built around discussions and activities. You will be doing most of the talking.

In each lesson we will start by reading and discussing a story. If you find it difficult to listen to the story because it is similar to something you have experienced, feel free to take some deep breaths, walk around the room, or do whatever makes you feel more comfortable.

Certain conversations may deserve longer time than we have. We encourage those conversations to continue after the session.

DISCUSSION

(10 min) Large group. Discuss the questions below. Then record the answers to Question 2 on a flip chart or large piece of paper, to post in the room. (If your group is large, do Question 1 in small groups, then get feedback in the large group).

1. What are your hopes and expectations for this group?
2. How can we make this group a safe place for everyone?

If participants do not suggest the following commitments, be sure to encourage them:

- We will keep each other's stories confidential (see page 190, Confidentiality).
- We will respect each other by not using phones or other electronics during meetings for any reason other than reading the Bible.
- We will not interrupt each other.
- We will give everyone a chance to speak.
- We will not give advice or solutions.
- We will start and end on time.

Note: It is recommended that no new participants be allowed to join the healing group after it begins and that visitors not be allowed, unless everyone in the group is in agreement that they may join. Trust and continuity of the lessons are important parts of experiencing the full healing process. So it is important that participants start with the group and come to all sessions. If someone has to miss a session, they should tell facilitators in advance if possible. Another person can go over materials with them before the next meeting.

1. If God loves us, why do we suffer?

Before you begin:

- For Section 1: Decide how you will present the story (see page 190, "Stories" in "Preparing the lessons").
- For Sections 2 and 3: If needed, prepare slips of paper or index cards with the Bible verses or use the Bible verses download.
- For Section 3A: If using a board or flip chart, make a table titled "God is," with two columns. Title the left column "Culture says" and the right column "Bible says."

God is	
Culture says	Bible says

- For Section 3B: Prepare the Radio skit, either with your co-facilitator or with volunteers from the group.
- For Section 4: Decide whether you will use the Word Art activity or the "Experiencing God's Love" exercise. For the Word Art activity, get paper and markers (one set per small group).
- For this and all subsequent lessons, review the Scripture references beforehand, including those in parentheses. You may find that some of the extra verses are helpful during the discussions or to answer questions. Remember that it is not necessary to use all the verses during the session. If your group is not familiar with the Bible, you should plan to explain some of the background for the verses listed for discussion.

In this lesson we will:

- Explain how evil and suffering came into the world, according to the Bible.
- Identify cultural beliefs, teachings about God, and personal experiences that can make it difficult to believe in God's love when we suffer.
- Learn how to respond to doubts about God's love.
- Begin to experience God's love in the midst of suffering.

Section 1: Story	15 min
Section 2: Why is there evil and suffering in the world?	10 min
Section 3: When we are suffering, what can make it hard to believe in God's love?	70 min
Section 4: How can we remember God's love in times of suffering?	15–25 min
Closing	1 min
Total time (approximately)	**2 hours**

1. If God loves us, why do we suffer?

F | *(1 min) Introduce lesson title and objectives. Direct participants to the corresponding lesson in Healing the Wounds of Trauma.*

Section 1.

15 min

The story of Pastor Ben

F | *(5 min) Large group. Present the story.*

A little boy named Ben grew up in the city. His mother was not married but she did her best to look after Ben. When he was three years old, she died suddenly. It looked as though Ben would have to go into foster care, but his mother's sister, Anne, offered to take him in. She and her husband Dan already had three children, older than Ben, and Dan did not really want the responsibility of another child.

Ben was frightened and upset when he was taken to Anne and Dan's house, and he showed these feelings by behaving badly. Dan decided he needed discipline and often hit him, but that just made Ben's behavior worse. The other three children resented how much time their mother spent on Ben and bullied him when the adults were not around.

Things got a bit better when Ben started school. As Ben grew older, one of his friends invited him to come to his youth group at church. There Ben heard for the first time that Jesus had died for him and wanted to be his friend. After some weeks he prayed to receive Christ into his life.

As Ben was finishing high school, the youth pastor told him about an inexpensive Bible school. Ben spent three happy years there, then got a job pastoring a small church. Soon he married a lovely Christian girl, Julie, and eventually they had two sons.

Ben and Julie's house was near the church. After a few years they began seeing a significant increase in violence in the surrounding community. Several members of his congregation knew people that had been shot—including children. One of the girls in the church had been assaulted.

Ben was at the church one day preparing for an evening service when he got a call from his wife. His five-year-old son Peter had been hit by a stray bullet. By the time Ben got to the hospital, it was too late. The doctors were not able to save little Peter's life.

Today, Ben still believes in the Bible, but he keeps asking why God has let him and his community suffer. He is angry with God and feels that God has deserted him. Sometimes he thinks that maybe God is not strong enough to stop these things from happening. When he thinks of God as his Father, he cannot imagine a loving father. In his experience, he only knew a father who was absent and an uncle who beat him.

Back in high school, a number of his teachers had been atheists. In his heart, Ben knows that God is with him, but sometimes he wonders if his teachers were right. Other times, when he sees the terrible things some of the people do, he thinks that maybe God is punishing the whole community. In his sermons he emphasizes the judgment of God and he rarely talks about God's love.

When he preaches that God understands what we are going through and is with us, he feels like a hypocrite since God seems far away.

DISCUSSION

> F | *(5 min) Small group. Discuss. Have each group select someone to take notes and speak for the group. (If possible, have the group select a different person for each small group discussion going forward.)*

1. What is Ben feeling in his heart about God?
2. Why do you think Ben feels this way about God?
3. Have you ever felt like Ben?

> F | *(5 min) Large group. Get feedback from each small group. If the participants are using books, encourage them to keep them closed for the rest of the lesson.*

Section 2.   10 min

Why is there evil and suffering in the world?

> F | *(1 min) Large group. Present the paragraph below.*

Like Pastor Ben, when we suffer we may have many questions about the evil and suffering in the world. These are questions that humans have asked since the beginning of time. The Bible begins with, "In the beginning God created the heavens and the earth" (Genesis 1:1), and then lists all that God created. When he finished, God looked over all he had made, and said it was very good (Genesis 1:31). If it was all "very good," what changed all that? Let's briefly discuss what the Bible says.

DISCUSSION

> F | *(7 min) Large group. Discuss, then add content from A–C that was not mentioned. If you have limited time, just summarize the content.*

The Bible tells us some things about why there is evil and suffering in the world. Consider the following verses: 1 Peter 5:8–9, Genesis 3:6–7, Genesis 3:17–18

A. Satan
The Bible says that there is a supernatural evil being at work in the world, an enemy of God who is behind all wickedness (1 Peter 5:8–9; 1 John 3:8). He is a liar and a murderer who seeks to kill, steal, and destroy (John 8:44).

B. Choice
God created people with the freedom to choose good or evil. When Adam and Eve chose to disobey God, evil and death entered the world (Genesis 3:6–7). As a result, all of humanity now

experiences sin and death (Romans 5:12). Sometimes we suffer from the choices of others or from our own choices (Romans 3:10–18; 1 Peter 2:20–22).

C. Damaged creation

Nature has been impacted as a result of Adam and Eve's disobedience (Genesis 3:17–18). The whole creation is marked by decay and pain. While creation is still "very good," it groans to be set free from brokenness (Genesis 1:31; Romans 8:19–22).

DISCUSSION

F │ *(3 min) Large group. Discuss. Possible answers: God wants a relationship with people, not slaves; love requires giving the beloved choice.*

If there was a risk of evil entering the world, why did God still give us choice?

Section 3.   70 min

When we are suffering, what can make it hard to believe in God's love?

F │ *(1 min) Large group. Mention the section title. Present the paragraph below.*

We have talked about why there is evil and suffering in the world and that God did not cause it. Yet even knowing this, we still struggle to make sense of our experience. Our pain and confusion can make us doubt God's love. Let's talk about why that might be.

A. Some cultural beliefs

DISCUSSION

F │ *(5 min) Small groups or pairs. Discuss. "Culture" can be country, region, ethnicity, church, family, and so on. If appropriate, divide into groups according to culture.*

1. What does your culture tell you God is like, especially in times of suffering?

F │ *(8 min) Large group. Get feedback. Write it in the left column of your "God is" chart. Add content below that was not mentioned.*

Some cultural beliefs are the same as what we learn from the Bible and help us through times of suffering. But other beliefs may be different, just like we saw in the story. These cultural beliefs may come to mind when we suffer and cause us to doubt God's love.

DISCUSSION

F │ *(5 min) Small groups or pairs. Divide the verses among the groups for discussion.*

1. What do the following verses teach us about God in times of suffering?

2 Peter 3:9   Proverbs 6:16–19   Matthew 9:35–36

Psalm 34:18   Isaiah 53:3–4   Romans 8:35–39

> F | *(10 min) Large group. Get feedback. Write it in the right column of your "God is" chart. Add content below that was not mentioned. Look at the two lists: What is the same and what is different? Say, "When doubts arise about God's love, it can help us to look to Scripture to remind ourselves of who God is."*

God is all-powerful, but he is also patient. When we pray that God will stop a certain evil thing, and it continues, we must not think it is because God is weak or does not care. He is in control and hears our prayers. He is slow to act because he wants to give everyone time to repent (2 Peter 3:9). When the time is right, God will powerfully judge sin (Psalm 73:27).

    God hates evil and injustice. Not everything that happens is the perfect will of God (Proverbs 6:16–19; Genesis 6:5–6; Romans 1:18).

    Jesus looks for us when we are suffering and has compassion on us. Jesus went looking for people who were suffering (Matthew 9:35–36). He preached the Good News and healed people of all their diseases. He felt pity for them.

    God comforts us. God is close to the brokenhearted and comforts us when we suffer (Psalm 34:18; 2 Corinthians 1:3–5). He holds us in his arms (Isaiah 40:11). He comforts us with his Word (Psalm 119:50, 92).

    Jesus suffered and feels our pain. Jesus understands our suffering because he suffered on the cross (Isaiah 53:3–4; Matthew 27:46; Hebrews 12:2–3). He suffers with those who are suffering (Matthew 25:35–36).

    God still loves us. Sometimes when trouble comes, we think it means that God does not love us anymore. This is not true. Nothing can separate us from his love (Romans 8:35–39). God promises to always be with us, even when we suffer (Psalm 23:4–5; Hebrews 13:5b–6; Isaiah 43:1–2).

B. Certain teachings

> F | *(4 min) Large group. Present the sentence below, then do the skit.*

In addition to cultural beliefs, certain teachings can keep us from believing in God's goodness when we suffer.

Radio skit

Narrator: Susanna has just experienced trauma. Her five-year-old son was killed by a stray bullet. She is overwhelmed and decides to listen to Christian radio for encouragement. A radio pastor on the first station she finds says:

Radio: "Do you have sin in your life? God knows—and he punishes sin! Repent before you fall into the hands of an angry God."

Susanna: "Oh, I must have sinned. That's why this happened! God is angry with me. But what did I do? I don't know what to confess!"

Narrator: She decides to go to another station, where a radio pastor says:

Radio:	"Jesus said, 'Fast and pray!' How much have you prayed today? How much have you fasted this week? How much money have you given to the church? Redouble your efforts and God will be pleased with you. He will answer your prayers."
Susanna:	"Oh, I have not done enough to please God. I should have prayed for two hours each morning, not just one. I should have fasted two days a week, not just one. And I should have found a way to give more money to the church. Then God would have blessed me. My son would not have died."
Narrator:	She turns the dial once more and hears this:
Radio:	"Hallelujah! If you have faith like a grain of mustard seed, you can say to this mountain—move to the sea, and it will be moved. Dear ones, do you have faith? Move that mountain in your life!"
Susanna:	"Oh, if only I had had more faith, my son would not have died. It's all my fault!"

F | *(3 min) Large group. Discuss the skit with these questions:*

1. What teachings did you hear in the skit? How did those teachings make Susanna feel?
2. Have you heard other teachings that make it difficult to believe in God's goodness when we suffer?

DISCUSSION

F | *(5 min) Discuss the three teachings in small groups, pairs, or large group, depending upon time.*
(3 min) Large group. Get feedback. Add content following each teaching that was not mentioned.

What does the Bible say about the following teachings?

1. "God is angry and quick to punish." Compare with Lamentations 3:22–23 and 1 John 4:9–11.

Some preaching makes us picture God in heaven as angry and wanting to punish us. The Bible tells us that God gets angry and punishes sin, but it also tells us of his great love for us (Jeremiah 31:3).

2. "Suffering means we have not done enough to please God." Compare with Romans 5:8 and Titus 3:4–6.

We may be told that we are suffering because we have not been good enough to please God. God's love is not based on our behavior. He loved us before we turned to him (1 John 4:19). He continues to love us by grace, not because of what we do (Romans 3:23–24; Ephesians 2:8–9).

3. "God promises prosperity for everyone who believes." Compare with Philippians 1:29 and 2 Corinthians 1:8–10.

If we are taught that people who obey God will always be rich and healthy, we may feel that we have caused our own suffering by our lack of obedience and faith. The apostle Paul is a good example of someone who suffered a lot even though he was very obedient to God.

C. Certain experiences

F | *(1 min) Large group. Present the paragraph below.*

Certain experiences we have had can also make it hard for us to trust in God's love when we suffer. For example, if we have had bad experiences with the church or with our earthly parents.

1. If we have had bad experiences with the church

F | *(2 min) Large group. Present the paragraph below, then briefly facilitate the discussion on Matthew 5:13-16.*

Jesus commanded his followers to reflect the character of God, to challenge injustice, and to help those in need (Matthew 25:31–46; John 13:34–35; James 1:27). When the church does not do this, evil increases, and people may imagine that God is as unconcerned with injustice as those who claim to follow him (Matthew 5:13–16).

DISCUSSION

Consider Matthew 5:13–16 for a description of how God's people should be.

2. If we have had bad experiences with our earthly parents

F | *(2 min) Large group. Present the paragraph below. "Parents" can include other significant people/caregivers. Read one or both of the Bible references out loud.*

Children need to feel secure and protected from evil. If we have experienced difficult things as a child, we may find it difficult to trust God when we become adults. For example, if we grew up without a father or mother, or if our caregiver was often angry with us, then we may think God has abandoned us or that he is always angry with us, even though the Bible teaches us that God is a loving Father (John 16:27; Romans 8:14–17).

Fig. 1: A loving father

DISCUSSION IN PAIRS

F | *(8 min) Pairs. Discuss. When half the time has passed, tell participants to switch speakers. Feedback is not necessary.*

Think about your own father. As a child, did you experience his love? Consider the same with your mother and other adults who took care of you. How does your experience with your earthly parents affect your experience with your heavenly Father?

DISCUSSION IN PAIRS OR SMALL GROUP

F | *(5 min) Pairs or small group. Feedback is not necessary.*

In the story, we heard about some of these barriers to God's love—some cultural beliefs, certain teachings, and certain experiences. Have any of these made it hard for you to trust that God loves you?

Section 4.   15–25 min

How can we remember God's love in times of suffering?

DISCUSSION

F | *(10 min) Large group. Discuss, then add content from A and B that was not mentioned.*

We cannot explain why God allows us to suffer. Even if we could, it would not take away the pain. What can we do to help ourselves remember God's love in times of suffering?

A. Recognize when we have experienced God's help and presence in painful situations.

When we suffer, we can think about how God has helped us in the past. We can also think of how God has delivered his people in the Bible when they suffered (Psalm 107:6, 13, 19, 28). This can bring us comfort (Psalm 77:2–3, 11–12).

B. Do the things that make our faith grow.

As we follow Jesus and study the Bible, we learn the truth about God, and this helps us become free from the lies of Satan (John 8:31–32; 2 Timothy 3:14–17). Christians need to meet together for teaching, prayer, and fellowship (Acts 2:42; Hebrews 10:24–25). If these things are missing, we will find it much harder to believe in God's goodness when we suffer.

C. Meditate on God's character.

F | *Select the option that best fits your context and the amount of time you have.*

WORD ART ACTIVITY

F | *(15 min) Introduce activity, then give 10 minutes to create and 5 minutes to share in pairs.*

What do you want to remember about God when you are suffering?

- Take a piece of paper and write "God" in the middle of the page. Surround the word "God" with words or drawings that summarize the characteristics of God that you want to remember when you are suffering.
- In pairs, share as much of your word art as you would like, or share what it was like to do this activity.

EXERCISE: EXPERIENCING GOD'S LOVE

F | *(5 min) Large group. Say, "I would like to lead you through an exercise that can help you experience God's love." Read the instructions and some of the verses, slowly and carefully, pausing between each verse. Leave silence at the end, for participants to reflect.*

It may be hard for you to receive love from God because you view him through the lens of your earthly parents. But God's pure and genuine love will not harm you. As you reflect on the following verses, they may help you get a better sense of how much God loves you.

Lamentations 3:21–24   1 John 3:1   Psalm 103:13
1 John 4:9–10   1 Peter 5:7

Closing   1 min

F | *(1 min) Give participants time to reflect on the question below. Close in prayer, incorporating one of the verses above. Encourage the participants to read the lesson and look up the Scripture passages after the session.*

What is one thing you want to remember from this lesson?

2. What is a wound of the heart?

Before you begin:

- For Section 1: Decide how you will present the story (see page 190, "Stories" in "Preparing the lessons").
- For Section 2A: Prepare the "physical wound/heart wound" chart, with the heart wound column blank. You can write just the bolded words, not complete sentences.
- For Section 3: If needed, prepare slips of paper or index cards with Bible verses or use the Bible verses download.
- For Section 3: Prepare "Bottles under water" materials.

In this lesson we will:

- Explain how trauma is a "heart wound" and identify how it makes people behave.
- Show that God accepts our honest emotions.
- Learn to manage strong feelings through a breathing exercise.

Section 1: Story	15 min
Section 2: What is a wound of the heart?	40 min
Section 3: What does the Bible teach us about expressing our feelings?	30 min
Closing	5 min
Total time	**1 hour 30 minutes**

2. What is a wound of the heart?

F | *(1 min) Introduce lesson title and objectives. Direct participants to the corresponding lesson in Healing the Wounds of Trauma.*

Section 1.   15 min

The fire

F | *(5 min) Large group. Present the story.*

It was three in the morning when the phone rang in Laurel and Pete's bedroom. Laurel looked sleepily at Pete as he answered it but became more alert as he started to get out of bed as he listened to the caller. "Bad fire," he said, "and it's coming this way!" Pete was a firefighter and Laurel was used to him being called out in the night, but somehow this seemed more serious than usual. Within five minutes Pete was out of the house on his way to the fire. Laurel wondered if she should wake the children, but first she went downstairs to turn on the television and find out what was happening.

Just as Laurel found a channel reporting on the fire, she heard cars driving outside, with loudspeakers telling everyone to get out. It took a while to get the three kids awake and dressed and into the car. As they left, clouds of smoke were getting nearer, and they could even see the fire in the distance. Finally, they arrived at a friend's house outside the danger zone. Laurel was so relieved to be safe, but then she began to worry about Pete.

There was no news for some hours but then Laurel got a message from a nearby hospital saying she should come at once because her husband was seriously hurt. As she rushed off, Laurel wondered if she would ever see Pete alive again. At the hospital, she heard that two other men in his unit had been killed and that Pete had burns on most of his body, his leg was crushed, and he had internal injuries. For three dreadful days, she thought he was going to die, but once they amputated his leg, he began to recover. It was a long time, though, before he could leave the hospital.

When he recovered, Pete was given a job in the office of the fire department. Laurel felt that things should be returning to normal, but now each week has seemed worse than the last. They both are having trouble sleeping and often have nightmares. But the worst part of it for Laurel has been Pete's personality change. Before the fire, he was generally a happy and balanced guy, but now he gets angry over little things. The children are beginning to be scared of their father because he yells at them when they make any noise. Laurel knows Pete is hurting inside because of the loss of his leg, but he will not talk about it because he thinks men should be strong. His friends just behave as though nothing has happened, but for Pete, his whole life has changed.

Laurel is becoming more and more depressed. She has lost interest in eating. It is especially hard for her at church because she is angry at God for not protecting her husband. Was God not able to protect him? Did God not care? What happened? Their pastor preaches that people who have strong faith in God are always H-A-P-P-Y and full of joy. Laurel knows this is not how she feels.

Finally Laurel talks to her small group leader, Pat. As she talks, she begins to cry and cannot stop sobbing. It feels like pressure inside her has been released. Pat listens to Laurel tell what had happened. She asks Laurel to explain how she felt during the whole experience, and finally they talk about what the hardest part of the experience was for Laurel.

Laurel goes away feeling relieved. They have agreed to get together again for coffee the next week.

DISCUSSION

F | *(5 min) Small group. You can divide the parts of Question 1 among the various groups. Have each group select someone to take notes and speak for the group. (If possible, have the group select a different person for each small group discussion going forward.)*

1. Besides the loss of Pete's leg, what else has he lost? What has Laurel lost? What have their children lost?
2. Think of people you know. What are some things they have lost?

F | *(5 min) Large group. Get feedback. If using a board/flip chart, list answers to Question 1 in three columns. Possible answers: security, beauty, economic ability, faith, health, sleep, happy home life, friends, job. The goal is that participants see how much was affected by this one event.*

If the participants are using books, encourage them to keep them closed for the rest of the lesson.

Section 2.   40 min

What is a wound of the heart?

F | *(7 min) Mention the section title. Present the content below, including the discussion question. Draw the circle diagram on the board/flip chart and explain.*

Some experiences in life are very painful. They can cause deep suffering which lasts a long time. This is what we call "trauma." Trauma is a deep wound of the heart and mind that takes a long time to heal. It hurts every part of our lives: how we relate to others, how our body feels, what we think about, and how much we can trust God. It can make us feel separated from God and others. We may feel like we are no longer the same person as before.

Trauma can be caused by a single event, a prolonged event, or repeated events. It overwhelms us with intense fear, helplessness, or horror, and there is nothing we can do to stop it from happening.

DISCUSSION

What types of events can cause trauma?

F | *(Possible answers: threat of death, serious injury, sexual assault, accidents, abuse, betrayal)*

Our hearts can also be wounded, or traumatized, when we hear the details of someone else's experience of trauma, especially if that person is a close family member or friend. This is referred to as secondary trauma.

The diagram below shows that trauma always involves loss, but we can experience loss and grief without trauma (for example, after the expected death of an elderly parent). Not all emotional pain is trauma, and not all problem behaviors are the result of trauma.

A. A heart wound is like a physical wound.

Fig. 2.1: Trauma/grief diagram

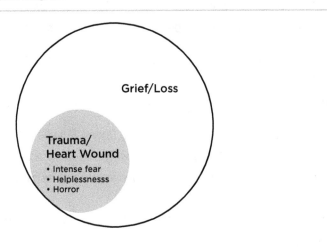

DISCUSSION

F | *(3 min) Large group.*

Think of a deep cut on your arm: How does it heal? What helps it heal?

F | *(10 min) Large group. Say, "Now let's compare a physical wound to a heart wound." Mention each item in the physical wound column and, as you do, ask, "Is this the same or different for a heart wound?"*
Then write "Same" in the heart wound column for items that are the same. If they are different, note how a heart wound is different from a physical wound.

Physical Wound	Heart Wound
It is **visible.**	It is invisible but shows up in the person's behavior.
It is **painful** and must be **treated with care.**	Same
If ignored, it is likely to get **worse.**	Same
It **must be cleaned** to remove any foreign objects or dirt.	The pain has to be expressed. If there is any sin, it must be confessed.
If a wound **heals on the surface** with infection still inside, it will cause the person to become **very sick.**	If people pretend their emotional wounds are healed when really they are not, it will often cause the person greater problems.
Only **God brings healing,** but often **uses people and medicine** to do so.	Same

Physical Wound	Heart Wound
If not treated, it often attracts **flies.**	Same. It often attracts bad things.
It **takes time to heal.**	Same
A healed wound **may leave a scar.**	Same. People can be healed, but they will not be exactly the same as before the wound.

B. How do people with wounded hearts behave?

F | *(15 min) Large group. Ask, "Who in our story had a wounded heart? How did they behave?" Get feedback. Then present the three behaviors below. Ask participants to give examples of each, then add the content that they did not mention. If people talk about these behaviors being caused by demons or ancestors, let them know this is not necessarily the case. See the footnote for an optional activity.*

When our hearts are wounded, it affects our lives. We may behave in three main ways: reliving the experience, avoiding reminders of the trauma, and being on alert all the time.

Reliving the experience
- thinking about the event all the time
- feeling like we are back in the event while awake (flashbacks) or asleep (nightmares)
- telling everyone about what happened over and over again

Any of these makes it hard to concentrate (at work or school).

Avoiding reminders of the trauma
- avoiding anything that brings back memories of the event (places, people)
- going numb, such as not caring about what happens to us, not being disturbed by violence or seeing dead bodies
- not remembering what happened, or only remembering parts of it
- using drugs, alcohol, pornography, work, food, or other addictive behaviors to avoid our feelings
- completely refusing to talk about it

Being on alert all the time
- always feeling tense, jumpy, frightened
- living in dread of another bad thing happening
- overreacting with violence or anger
- struggling to fall asleep, waking in the night, or waking early in the morning
- shaking, having a fast or irregular heartbeat
- having headaches and stomachaches
- feeling dizzy or faint, difficulty breathing, panic attacks

---

Optional activity

Have participants stand in a large circle. Ask, "If you know someone who has relived a trauma through nightmares or flashbacks, step into the circle." Then ask, "If you know someone who has tried to avoid memories of trauma through alcohol, drugs, overworking, overeating, and so forth, step into the circle." Finally, ask, "If you know someone who has been on alert all the time (jumpy, tense, overreacting, fast heartbeat, and so forth) after experiencing a traumatic event, step into the circle." This exercise helps the group see that these behaviors are normal and widespread.

C. What makes some wounds of the heart more serious?

F | *(5 min) Mention the section title, then present the content below, drawing out examples from the group.*

Some situations are more difficult than others. For example:
- Something that causes shame, the sense that we are very bad or deeply flawed.
- Something that forces us to act in ways that go against our beliefs about what is right, especially if others have been harmed in the process. (This is often called a moral injury.)
- Something very personal, for example, a family member dying or being betrayed by a close friend.
- Something that goes on for a long time.
- Something that happens many times over a period of time.
- Something that causes an unexpected death.
- Something that people have done intentionally to cause us pain rather than something that is accidental.

People react to painful events differently. Two people may go through the same event, but one may have a severe reaction while the other is not affected much at all. A person is likely to react more severely if he or she:
- has mental illness or emotional problems.
- is usually sad or is highly sensitive.
- had many bad things happen in the past, especially as a child, like being abused or having both parents die.
- already had many problems before this happened.
- did not have the support of family or friends during and after the event.

Section 3.

30 min

What does the Bible teach us about expressing our feelings?

F | *(3 min) Mention the section title. Briefly discuss the question, then present the content below it.*

DISCUSSION

What does your culture teach people to do with their emotions when they are suffering inside?

Some Christians who have troubles say that we should not think or talk about our feelings. They also say that we should not go to others for help with our troubles. They say we should just forget the past and move on. Or, they say we should only pray about it and read the Bible. They think that feeling pain in our hearts means we are doubting God's promises. This is not true!

DISCUSSION

F | *(5 min) Small group. Divide the verses among the groups.*

As you read the verses below, consider the following questions:

1. What is happening?
2. How are people expressing their feelings?

Matthew 26:37–38 (Jesus)	John 11:33–35 (Jesus)
Matthew 26:75 (Peter)	Jonah 4:1–3 (Jonah)
1 Samuel 1:10, 13–16 (Hannah)	Psalm 55:4–6 (David)

F | *(15 min) Large group. To get feedback, have each group read or summarize their passage and their discussion. Then ask, "Can we safely say that God welcomes the honest expression of our feelings?" Add content below that was not mentioned.*

Jesus had strong feelings and shared them with his disciples. Paul teaches us to share our problems with each other as a way of caring for each other (Galatians 6:2; Philippians 2:4). The Old Testament is full of examples of people pouring out their hearts to God: for example, Hannah, David, Solomon, Jeremiah. The psalmist told God, "My heart is wounded within me" (Psalm 109:22b, NIV). God wants us to be honest and speak the truth from our hearts (Psalm 15:1–2).

F | *(7 min) Do the "Bottles under water" exercise (see footnote).*

Closing

5 min

F | *(5 min) Lead the participants through the breathing exercise, then give them time to reflect on Question 2. Encourage the participants to read the lesson and look up the Scripture passages after the session. Note: Some people can panic when they do a breathing exercise. Make sure people know that this exercise is not mandatory.*

Bottles under water exercise

Start by saying, "Here is an activity to show what happens when we try to hold painful feelings inside."

Get a basin full of water and five or six empty water bottles. Each bottle represents a pain. Have everyone gather around and talk about the different pains as you put each bottle in the water. Try to hold all the bottles underwater at the same time. As the number of bottles increases, it will be harder and harder to hold them all down. Say, "It takes a lot of effort to hold the bottles down. In the same way, keeping pain insides takes a lot of effort. We are not able to pay attention to things like sermons, school, work, and so forth."

Eventually some of the water bottles will pop to the surface of the water, because you will not be able to hold them all down. Let the bottles surface and ask, "What does this teach us about trying to hold in our emotions?"

Variation, if it is not possible to use bottles and water: Ask a volunteer to name an event that evoked emotions (like anger) and give them an object to hold (such as a pencil). Then keep naming events that cause different kinds of emotions, adding a different object each time for them to hold. It is best if the objects are different shapes and sizes. Objects from the group table can be used. Eventually the person will not be able to hold all the items. Ask, "What does this teach us about trying to hold all of our emotions?"

1. Breathing exercise

   Breathing deeply can help us relax when we feel strong emotions. If this makes you feel uncomfortable at any point, you can stop. You are in control.
   - Get into a comfortable sitting position.
   - Close your eyes if you like or pick a spot on the wall and concentrate on it. Think only about your breathing.
   - Slowly breathe in and out, filling your lungs and slowly releasing the air. Think to yourself, "(Your name), feel yourself relaxing as breath is flowing in and out."
   - Think about being in a quiet place. It might be the beach, or on a hill or in a tree. You might be alone or with someone who cares for you. You might think about Jesus telling you how much he loves you.
   - Continue to think about your breathing, flowing in and out, in and out.
   - After a few minutes, open your eyes or release your gaze from the spot on the wall. Stretch and take one more deep breath.
2. What is one thing you want to remember from this lesson?

F | *If desired, after this lesson and before the next, you may insert the lesson on Moral Injury.*

3. What can help our heart wounds heal?

Before you begin:

- For Section 1: Decide how you will present the story (see page 190, "Stories" in "Preparing the lessons").
- For Section 2B: Find 1–2 volunteers to prepare the Listening skit.
- For Section 2C: Find out about the services available in the area for people with heart wounds who may need additional support.
- For Section 3: Get supplies for the art exercise.

In this lesson we will:

- Care for heart wounds by talking and listening.
- Care for heart wounds by doing an art exercise.

Section 1: Story	15 min
Section 2: How can talking about our pain help us heal?	60 min
Section 3: How else can we express our pain?	43 min
Closing	2 min
Total time	**2 hours**

3. What can help our heart wounds heal?

F | *(1 min) Introduce lesson title and objectives. Direct participants to the corresponding lesson in Healing the Wounds of Trauma.*

Section 1.   **15 min**

The school trip

F | *(5 min) Large group. Present the story.*

Helen and Richard were sitting at home enjoying a peaceful evening with their youngest daughter, Ruth. The two older children, Charlie and Alice, were away on a school trip to the coast to study in a wildlife reserve. Helen's phone rang, and she saw it was a call from the mother of a child in Charlie's class. When she answered the phone, she could hardly understand what this mother was saying. The woman was crying and screaming, but finally Helen understood that something had happened to the children on their way to the wildlife reserve. After a number of frantic phone calls, Helen and Richard discovered that the children's bus had fallen off a bridge.

They left Ruth with a neighbor and jumped in their car. When they arrived at the accident, they found a scene of confusion—police cars with flashing lights, ambulances leaving with sirens blaring, parents pressing in and trying to find out what had happened to their children. Finally, they were told gently by a police woman that both their children had been killed and had been taken to the morgue.

Three months later, Richard seemed to be coping and was trying to help their little daughter Ruth. Helen, however, had sunk into a deep depression. She did not want to eat, was not cooking meals for the family any more, and had not returned to her work as a teacher. They were both Christians, and their church had tried hard to help them, bringing meals and sending cards, but Helen had not been to church since the tragedy.

One afternoon Sue, an older woman in the church, came to visit Helen. No one from church up to this point had talked with her about what had happened. They avoided all mention of the children who had died. Sue, however, asked Helen, "What exactly happened the day the bus crashed?" Helen explained all about the bridge and how most of the children had died when the bus dropped twenty feet. Helen found it was a relief to talk about it. Then Sue asked, "How did you feel?" Helen was quiet and then started to explain her feelings of panic and despair when she was at the accident site, and the dark cloud that had enveloped her ever since.

Finally, Sue asked, "What was the hardest part for you?" Helen was quick to reply. "The feeling of guilt," she said. "We should never have let them go on this trip." As she said this out loud, something opened inside of her, and she cried and cried as Sue held her. This was the beginning of her long journey of healing.

DISCUSSION

F | (5 min) Small group. Ask Question 1 to the large group, to identify the three listening questions. Then divide those three questions among the small groups, to discuss how each question helped. Have each group select someone to take notes and speak for the group. (If possible, have the group select a different person for each small group discussion going forward.)

1. What three questions did Sue ask Helen?
2. How did each of these questions help Helen?

F | (5 min) Large group. Get feedback. If the participants are using books, encourage them to keep them closed for the rest of the lesson.

Section 2.   60 min

How can talking about our pain help us heal?

F | (1 min) Mention the section title, then present the paragraph below.

One way we get pain out of our hearts is by talking about it. Even if we talk to God about our bad experiences, telling another person about what happened is an important part of healing. As we share our pain with another person, little by little our reactions will become less and less intense. We may need to tell our story many times. But if we are not able to talk about our pain, and if there is no one to listen to us, these reactions may continue for months and even years.

A. What begins to happen when we talk about our pain?

F | (1 min) Present the content below.

When we talk with someone who listens well, it can help us:
*   gain an honest understanding of what happened and how it has affected us.
*   express our feelings about what happened.
*   accept what happened.
*   feel heard and know we are not alone.
*   trust that God also wants to hear about our pain (Psalm 62:8).

B. What is a good listener like?

F | (1 min) Present the content below.

We can help each other heal by listening to each other. This requires that we become good listeners. What is a good listener like?

F (10 min) Say, "First let's watch a skit, and then we will talk about it." Have pre-selected participants act out the skit. Ensure that participants who are watching the skit have their books closed so they do not know how it will end.

Listening skit

Narrator: Michael (or Mary) was in a bad car accident a week ago. It left him (or her) with a broken arm and a minor concussion, nearly killed his (her) spouse and child, and killed the driver of the other car. He (she) has been able to go home from the hospital but is worried about his (her) family. Although he (she) has people to help with meals, and so on, he (she) is feeling worse and worse. His (her) pastor has just stopped at the hospital to visit. The pastor finds Michael (Mary) in the waiting area, pacing back and forth.

(P = Pastor; M = Michael/Mary)

Skit 1

P: (rushed greeting) I came to see your family.

M: They're sleeping just now, but I'm not doing so well.

P: (rushed) Look at the **positive**: you survived! Thank God!

M: But I'm feeling **confused**. Could we talk?

P: (distracted) I have a building committee meeting. Let's talk as we walk to my car.

M: Okay (reluctantly). Now that my wife (husband) and daughter are okay, I'm **feeling worse**. I'm **not sleeping** and I'm **avoiding cars** and especially driving.

P: There's **no reason to be afraid**. Forget it. **Take control**. God hasn't given us a "spirit of fear."

M: Oh no! Now I feel **guilty** about feeling **afraid**. And I feel angry. I know I should feel **thankful**, but …

P: Yes! You should be thankful. Being thankful will wipe away the negative feelings. **This reminds me** of when our church burned down. I decided to rejoice, and everything was fine.

M: I tried to but I **can't control the fear**. (P's phone rings)

P: (answers his phone and says) "I'm talking with Michael (Mary). He's (she's) having a really hard time, but I'll be there as soon as I can get away."

M: I can see you're busy, but what can I do about this fear?

P: Remember **Romans 8:28**. Be thankful. **I'll ask the church to pray** for you.

M: Oh please no, don't tell everyone!

P: Don't worry—we're a **family**. It's all in the family. There's no reason to be embarrassed. I've gotta run.

M: (dejected)

F Ask, "What did you see happening in this skit?" Discuss.

Skit 2

P: (greeting) I came to see you.

M: Thanks! I'm not doing so well.

P: Do you want to talk? Let's go somewhere private.

M: Okay.

P: **Tell me what happened.**

M: It's a **horrible scene in my head**. We were on the way to the airport and going up a hill, when a car came over the hill into our lane, speeding. There was no time to react. I swerved and spun and ended up in a ditch upside down. My wife (husband) and daughter were unconscious and bleeding. I got out and was screaming for my family. I managed to get them out from under the car. I was afraid the gas would explode.

P: It's **amazing you could think clearly**. Were you in pain?

M: I don't know. It was a blurry nightmare. I think I was in shock.

P: **How did you feel?**

M: Well, first I was glad to have survived, but now I have bad thoughts and feelings. I'm confused. I **felt so helpless** and **wanted to kill the driver**. He died, but I wish I could have killed him myself. I shouldn't feel this way.

P: **I'd probably feel that way, too.**

M: **Really? Helpful to hear.** I'm not sleeping well. I know cars are probably safe, but I'm afraid of them anyway. I'm feeling very angry for no reason. I should feel thankful my family is recovering, right?

P: Well, it's normal to have all these feelings after what you've been through. **What was the hardest thing for you?**

M: The worst was seeing my daughter and wife (husband) injured.

P: Yeah. You said you felt helpless?

M: Totally. I'm responsible to take care of my family, and I couldn't do anything.

P: **What helped you cope so far?**

M: My family needs me.

P: Yeah. We love you too. We can talk again soon, okay?

M: Thanks. It **really helps to talk about it**. Do you want to see my family? They're awake now.

P: Yes, let's.

> F | *Ask, "What did you see happening in this skit?" Discuss.*

DISCUSSION

> F | *(12 min) Large group. Discuss, then add content below that was not mentioned.*

With what kind of person would you feel free to share your deep pain?

Fig. 3.1: A good listener

1. A good listener creates a safe space.

- Cares about you.
- Finds a safe and quiet place where you can talk without interruption.
- Does not force you to share more than you are comfortable sharing.
- Does not criticize you, preach at you, or give you quick solutions (Proverbs 18:13).
- Listens and understands your pain (Proverbs 20:5).
- Does not minimize your pain by comparing it with his or her own.
- Keeps the information confidential (Proverbs 11:13; 20:19).

2. A good listener asks helpful questions.

F | *Write the three questions on a board, flip chart, or large paper.*

Here are three helpful questions a good listener might use:

1. What happened?
2. How did you feel?
3. What was the hardest part for you?

F | *Rationale for the three questions:*
| *Q1: Helps you sort out facts and timeline, which get jumbled in your brain during a*
| *traumatic event.*
| *Q2: Since healing takes place at the level of emotions, it helps to name them.*
| *Q3: This helps you identify your deepest pain. It also guards the listener from thinking*
| *they already know the answer.*

A good listener lets you speak at your own pace. Your answers to the three questions may come out naturally. It may take several meetings to discuss the whole story.

3. A good listener shows he or she is listening.

- Looks at you (if that is good in the culture), not out the window, at their watch, or at their phone.
- Does not seem impatient for you to finish.
- Says words of agreement like "Mmm."

- From time to time, repeats what they think you have said so you can correct, restate, or affirm their understanding.

4. A good listener respects the healing process.
- Notices if you become very distressed. Lets you take a break, think about other things, and get calm inside. Allows you to resume telling your story when you feel ready.
- May ask if you would like prayer. If you say "yes," the listener prays but does not preach. If you are not ready to pray together, the listener honors this.

C. What are signs that someone may need additional help?

F | *(5 min) Present the content below. Discuss what services are available in the area to get the additional support to people who need it.*

Here are signs that someone may need more help beyond spending time with a good listener:
- Their behaviors put life and health at risk.
- They are unable to complete daily activities or care for basic needs.
- They frequently cannot manage their emotions.
- They think things are happening that are not real, such as hearing voices or imagining that they are being followed.

These behaviors show that someone needs professional help. If a psychologist or psychiatrist is not available, a doctor or nurse may at least give them medicine to calm them down and help them sleep.

LISTENING EXERCISE, IN PAIRS

F | *(20 min) Read the instructions below and have participants do the exercise in pairs. Give 10 minutes for each participant.*

We become good listeners by practicing. Even as we practice, we can help each other heal. In groups of two, talk about one painful thing that happened to you—a small thing, not the worst thing you have experienced. The other person listens, using the three questions below. Then switch roles.

1. What happened?
2. How did you feel?
3. What was the hardest part for you?

F | *(10 min) Large group. Discuss the questions below.*
1. How did you feel during this exercise?
2. Was anything difficult when you were the listener? Explain.
3. Was anything difficult when you were sharing? Explain.
4. What did the listener do well?

Section 3.

How else can we express our pain?

F | *Present the paragraph below.*

Another way we can express the pain in our hearts is by doing activities such as drawing, poetry, dance, and music. Each of our cultures has different ways that people express themselves. We can use some of these ways to help find healing for our hearts.

ART EXERCISE

F | *(23 min) Present the paragraph below, to describe the art exercise. Then give participants 20 minutes to create. Participants can use markers, colored pencils, clay, chalk, movement, spoken word, song, and so forth.*

Start by getting quiet inside and asking God to show you the pain in your heart. It may be pain from something about your life today or something from the past. When you are ready, you can begin expressing your pain through the art form you have chosen. Your artistic expression may be symbolic rather than realistic. This exercise is not about showing artistic talent to others, but about expressing what is in your heart.

DISCUSSION

F | *(15 min) Small groups or pairs.*

1. Share as much or as little as you like about what you have created. Or, if you prefer, share what the experience was like of expressing your pain in this way.
2. Did you realize anything new?
3. Pray for one another.

F | *(5 min) Large group. Ask if anyone would like to share about what they created.*

Closing

F | *(2 min) Give participants time to write down or share their answers to this question. Encourage the participants to read the lesson and look up the Scripture passages after the session.*

What is one thing you want to remember from this lesson?

4. What happens when someone is grieving?

Before you begin:

- For Section 1: Decide how you will present the story (see page 190, "Stories" in "Preparing the lessons").
- For Section 3: Prepare the Grief Journey skit and draw the grief journey on board, flip chart, or large paper.
- Plan a short break before beginning the lament section.
- Get extra paper for the lament exercise.
- If desired, select a lament psalm to read during the closing.
- Translators: Find a word for "grieving" that can include all kinds of grief, not just mourning the death of a person. If there is not a word available, expand the sense of the grief word to include mourning the loss of other things.

In this lesson we will:

- Recognize the different stages of grief.
- Discuss how to respond well to the grieving process in our own lives and in the lives of others.
- Express our pain to God through lament as an important part of grieving.

Section 1: Story	10 min
Section 2: What is grieving?	5 min
Section 3: How can we grieve in a way that brings healing?	35 min
Section 4: What can make grieving more difficult?	10 min
Section 5: How can we help each other grieve?	15 min
Laments	40-55 min
Closing	5 min
Total time	**2 hours - 2 hours 15 minutes**

4. What happens when someone is grieving?

F │ *(1 min) Introduce lesson title and objectives. Direct participants to the corresponding lesson in Healing the Wounds of Trauma.*

Section 1.

10 min

The night that changed Tony's life

F │ *(5 min) Large group. Present the story.*

Tony lived in a cramped one-bedroom apartment with his two younger brothers and his mom. He worked part time, went to school full time, and had goals to finish high school and make a good life for himself and his family. He worked hard to stay out of trouble and to avoid the mistakes that so many of his friends had made.

One night, Tony took an extra shift at the pizza place where he worked, so he did not get home until almost midnight. He saw five missed calls and voice message from his mom, and he knew something was terribly wrong. His whole body went numb as he listened to his mom's shaky voice calling from the hospital to tell him what happened.

A shooting had occurred right in front of Tony's house. His mom was on her way home with his brothers and they found themselves in the middle of it. His youngest brother was shot and killed immediately, and Joe, his other brother, was seriously wounded and taken to the hospital.

Weeks after the youngest brother's funeral, Joe returned home from the hospital in a wheelchair. Tony's grief began to overwhelm him. He found himself crying when he least expected it. This made him feel embarrassed and he tried hard to hold in his feelings. He began losing sleep and was tormented with thoughts of guilt and regret. "If only I had been there, I could have stopped it!" Over and over again these thoughts ran through his mind. He also became obsessed with getting justice for his family. Before long, he got an F on a test in algebra—a first for him. His boss threatened to fire him because he was making so many mistakes on the job. Tony's mom became withdrawn and unable to care for the two boys. They began acting out in school and were on the verge of being expelled. Every night there was shouting in their apartment.

DISCUSSION

F | *(5 min) Large group.*

1. What is Tony experiencing?
2. What are some of the different ways people in the story behaved after losing a loved one?
3. Have you ever felt like Tony?

F | *If the participants are using books, encourage them to keep them closed for the rest of the lesson.*

Section 2.

5 min

What is grieving?

DISCUSSION

F | *(4 min) Large group. Define grief (feeling deep sorrow about the loss of someone or something). Discuss the question below. Then add content below the question that was not mentioned. Draw the "trauma/grief" diagram again (Heart wounds lesson).*

What kinds of losses do we grieve?

Grieving is feeling deep sorrow about the loss of someone or something. This might be the loss of a family member or a friend. It might be the loss of a body part or the function of part of the body. It might be the loss of property or position or hope. Whether small or large, all losses affect us (Nehemiah 1:3–4). Grieving is the normal process of recovering from these losses. Trauma always involves loss, but we can experience loss without trauma, as in the case of the slow death of an elderly parent.

When people lose someone or something very important to them, they may lose a sense of who they are. For example, they are no longer the wife of _____, or the mother of _____, or the president of _____. Their life will never be the same. Through the grieving process, a person's former sense of who they are will change. This takes time.

Because Adam and Eve sinned, death and loss came into the world. Only in heaven will there be no more mourning (Revelation 21:4). Christians can grieve and have hope at the same time (1 Thessalonians 4:13).

INDIVIDUAL REFLECTION

F | *(1 min) Give participants time to reflect on the question.*

What kinds of losses have you experienced?

How can we grieve in a way that brings healing?

> F | *(20 min) Present the paragraph below, then present the Grief Journey skit (see footnote). Some facilitators prefer to present the descriptions of the three neighborhoods first, drawing out examples from the participants, before leading participants through the skit.*

Grieving takes time and energy (Psalm 6:6–7). It is often like a journey that takes us through several neighborhoods. Each person spends different amounts of time in the neighborhoods and goes back and forth at different times. Understanding the grief journey does not take away the pain, but it can help us be more patient with ourselves and others. If we allow ourselves to take the journey, it will lead to healing.

Fig. 4.1: The journey of grief

A. The Neighborhood of Denial and Anger

> F | *Say, "Immediately after the disaster, the family is in Neighborhood 1, the Neighborhood of Denial and Anger. This often lasts 1 month or longer." Present the content below.*

Grief Journey skit

Mark the neighborhoods of Denial and Anger, No Hope, and New Beginnings with signs at three places in the room. You can put the signs on the wall or on chairs or have one person or a group of people hold a sign at each neighborhood.

The size of your group will affect how this skit is done. If your group is large, have five people come to the front of the room, and have the other participants stand at the three neighborhoods. If your group is small, have all the participants come to the front of the room.

State an imaginary disaster to the participants at the front of the room, for example, they are a family whose mother/wife has just died in a car accident. Then follow the facilitator prompts in A–F. Use participant names instead of "Person A, B, C, etc." (If you prefer, you can also have the participants think of a loss they have experienced and act out what they were feeling and saying at each neighborhood).

People will remember this grief journey more if they dramatize the different thoughts and emotions. If the people are shy and hesitant, the facilitator should lead in acting the anger, denial, and so on at each neighborhood; usually the participants join in readily.

Right after a loss, denial and anger are natural and can actually be helpful:

- Denial allows us to absorb the loss little by little and keeps us from being overwhelmed by it.
- Anger can be a way of fighting against the loss when we feel helpless. It can give us energy and keep us from being overwhelmed.

F | *Ask, "How would you describe people in the Neighborhood of Denial and Anger?" Get responses. Add content below that was not mentioned. Explain that the behavior is normal in each neighborhood as a person goes from crisis to recovery.*

Common responses:

- Numbness
- Unaware of what is happening around us
- Cannot believe the person has died or the event has happened
- May suddenly start to cry or erupt in anger
- Angry with God
- Angry with a person who has died, for leaving us alone
- "If only I had done this or that, the person wouldn't have died" or "I wish I had …"
- "Why did this happen to me?"
- May find someone to blame for the death
- May take revenge, which results in conflict and more pain
- May think we hear or see the dead person

F | *Say (and act), "Persons A and B are very angry at the people who caused the event and want revenge now! They get angry with anyone who walks in the room and shout at them. (Encourage A and B to act in this way, and so on, with the description of each subsequent person.) C is very angry at himself because he thinks he could have prevented the disaster. D is very angry at God for permitting this to happen. E is saying that the loved one is not really dead, they will be reunited soon." Present the paragraph below.*

This stage can begin during the time of the funeral or immediately after the loss, and while people are still coming to comfort the bereaved family. Weeping and rituals of the wake and burial are often helpful.

B. The Neighborhood of No Hope

F | *Say, "At a certain point, we may come to Neighborhood 2, the Neighborhood of No Hope. This often lasts between 6–15 months, although it can be different for each person." Present the sentences below.*

Neighborhood 2 is the darkest place in the grieving process. People do not expect anything good to follow.

F | *Ask, "How would you describe the people in the Neighborhood of No Hope?" Get responses. Add content below that was not mentioned. Explain that the behavior is normal in each neighborhood as a person goes from crisis to recovery.*

Common responses:
- Sad and hopeless
- Unable to organize life
- Longing for the dead person to come back
- Lonely
- Suicidal
- Guilty even if there is no reason to
- Avoiding the pain with drugs or other addictions

F   *Say (and act), "Person A stays in Denial and Anger because he/she is still very angry and thinking about revenge. (Encourage A to act in this way, and so on, with the description of each subsequent person.) B, C, and D no longer feel as much anger and they go to the camp of No Hope. B does not want to get out of bed, C is drinking alcohol, D is suicidal. E finally accepts that the love one is dead and goes to No Hope. Suddenly C sees something that reminds him/her of the initial event, and that triggers more anger. (Facilitator walks back with C to Denial and Anger to join A.)"*

   Say, "After a few weeks Persons A and C find that their anger is calming down, and they join the others at No Hope. They all feel sad, they are not interested in life."

C. The Neighborhood of New Beginnings

F   *Say, "At a certain point, we may come to Neighborhood 3, the Neighborhood of New Beginnings." Present the paragraph below.*

In Neighborhood 3, people increasingly accept the loss and their new identity. What is "normal" now is different—a "new normal." They may be more aware of what really matters in life. If they have grieved well, they may be able to help others.

F   *Ask, "How would you describe people in the Neighborhood of New Beginnings?" Get responses. Add content below that was not mentioned.*

Common responses:
- Thinking about moving on to a new life
- Ready to go out and enjoy time with friends
- Considering remarrying if a spouse died, or having another child if a child died
- Changed by the loss; may be stronger, more tender

F   *Say (and act), "Ten months after the crisis, D and E start to feel more interest in life. They go to New Beginnings. D wants to spend time with friends. E wants to look for a job. (Encourage D and E to act in this way, and so on, with the description of each subsequent person.) They start to join in activities with their friends. But A, B, and C still feel sad and lonely in No Hope. Twelve months after the disaster, B and C also go to New Beginnings. But A stays in No Hope, still longing for the person who died. On Christmas, however, B, C, and D have painful memories of how Christmas used to be, and they go for a time back to No Hope. Then, at about a year they all move to New Beginnings to join E."*

Say, "Every one of the five people's journeys was different. Each individual spends different amounts of time in the neighborhoods and goes back and forth at different times."

D. The grief journey is not always direct.

F | *Present the content below.*

It is normal to revisit previous neighborhoods for short periods of time. Sometimes this happens in response to an event like the anniversary of a death. Gradually a person moves more and more into the Neighborhood of New Beginnings.

Sometimes people get stuck too long in Neighborhood 1 or 2 and may need special help to move on. Examples of this might be:

- A woman who still thinks she can see or hear her husband years after he died.
- A mother of a dead child who keeps his clothes ready for him and will not give them away a year or more after the death.
- A man who is still unwilling to go to social events with his friends two years after his wife has died.

E. The false bridge

F | *Say, "Now a different disaster has just happened to Person A." (Place Person A at the moment of the crisis.)*

Say, "What if someone comes at the time of the crisis and takes the hand of A and tries to pull him/her toward New Beginnings, saying, 'Don't be angry, don't be sad. If you trust God, you can feel happy right now. Just resume your life as though nothing has happened'?" (Act this out with A, pulling him or her along toward Neighborhood 3. Have A fall down before you arrive at Neighborhood 3, collapsing on the ground.) Ask, "Does this work?" (No)

Present the content below. Add the false bridge to your grief journey drawing.

Sometimes we think that since we believe the gospel and all the promises of God, it would be wrong to feel angry or sad about a loss. Our cultures may reinforce this idea. This can be called the "false bridge," because it appears to provide a straight path from the moment of the loss directly to "New Beginnings" without passing through Neighborhoods 1 and 2. This is not biblical, and it will not bring healing.

God made us with the need to grieve our losses. Jesus expressed painful emotions on the cross when he said, "My God, my God, why did you abandon me?" (Matthew 27:46). The psalmist cried to God day and night when he was in exile, remembering all he had lost (Psalm 42:3–6).

Facing the pain of loss takes courage. We are tempted to avoid it. Sometimes we get busy doing God's work as a way to avoid feeling the pain. But if we do not grieve a loss, the grief will stay in us and may cause problems for many years.

Fig. 4.2: The false bridge

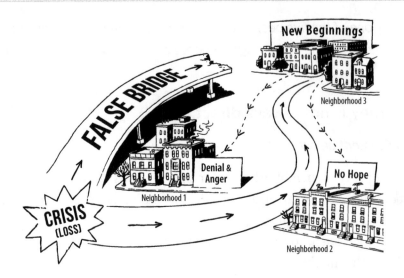

F. Sometimes the grief journey is delayed.

F | *Present the content below. Introduce the Container exercise here, if appropriate (Caregiver lesson).*

Sometimes it is necessary to set aside losses in order to survive. The context might require us to just keep going or keep working, for example, because of responsibilities or because it is not safe to talk about the issue. When we are safe and life is stable again, we will need to take the grief journey. As we saw in the "Bottles under water" exercise, it takes effort to keep the emotions buried inside us.

DISCUSSION IN PAIRS

F | *(10 min) Pairs. See footnote for an alternative to this discussion.*

Think of a loss you have experienced.

1. What was your grief journey like?
2. Did you loop back or get stuck along the way?
3. Did you try to take the false bridge?
4. Did you have to delay the journey?

F | *(5 min) Large group. Get feedback.*

ALTERNATIVE TO DISCUSSION IN PAIRS *(15 min)*

Get 4–5 pieces of large paper. Label the papers with the following headings: Denial and Anger, No Hope, New Beginning, the False Bridge, Delaying the Journey (if appropriate). Put each paper on a different table, with some art supplies.

Say, "Think of a loss you have experienced. What was your grief journey like? Take time at each table and express your feelings or thoughts on the paper, in words, colors, or a drawing. For example, write in words or draw a picture of what you felt or thought when you were in the Neighborhood of No Hope. Feel free to start at any table." (If everyone tries to work on the stages in order, there may be too many people at one table.)

Post the papers on the wall or take time for participants to see what others have expressed.

Section 4.

What can make grieving more difficult?

F | *(1 min) Mention the section title and present the paragraph below.*

Grieving is hard work, but some things can make it even more difficult. These can be things such as how the loss happened, beliefs people have about grief, and people who say or do things that show they do not understand.

A. The type of loss

F | *(2 min) Say, "Some losses are especially difficult, such as when a child has died. What other types of losses are especially difficult?" Get feedback, then add content below that was not mentioned.*

- When there are many deaths or losses at the same time
- When the death or loss is sudden or violent, for example, suicide or murder
- When there is no corpse to be buried or no way to confirm that the person has died
- When you are displaced and cannot participate in the grieving rituals
- When a provider or leader has died
- When the bereaved have unresolved problems with the dead person
- When a child has died

B. Beliefs about weeping

DISCUSSION

F | *(4 min) Large group. Discuss, then add content below that was not mentioned.*

1. What does your culture or family say about men weeping? About women weeping?
2. In what ways do these beliefs help or hinder people's grieving?

Some cultures require people to cry publicly when someone dies. Those who do not cry are suspected of not caring about the person who died, or of having caused the death. This can result in people crying dramatically, whether they feel sad or not.

Other cultures do not allow people to cry, especially men. This can result in people holding their grief inside rather than expressing it.

People should not hold their tears inside. God has designed us to cry or weep when we are sad. It is an important part of grieving, for men as well as women. Even Jesus wept when his close friend Lazarus died (John 11:33–38a). The psalmists wept (Psalm 6:6; Psalm 39:12; Psalm 42:3), as did the prophets (Isaiah 22:4; Jeremiah 9:1).

God notices our tears; they are precious to him (Isaiah 38:3–5; Psalm 56:8).

C. Miserable comforters

DISCUSSION

F | *(3 min) Large group. Discuss briefly, then add content below that was not mentioned.*

1. Do you know the story of Job in the Bible? What do you remember about it?
2. What did Job's friends do or say that was helpful?
3. What did they do or say that was not helpful?

Job was a wealthy man with a large family. In an instant, he lost everything: his children, his cattle, his wealth, his health. When three of Job's friends heard what happened to him, they got together and went to comfort him (Job 2:11). They sat in silence with him for a week before speaking. When Job broke the silence and expressed his pain, his friends were quick to point out his lack of faith (Job 4:3–6). They said his suffering was due to his sins and the sins of his children (Job 4:7–8). Although Job claimed he had not sinned, they were sure that if he were innocent God would not have let this happen (Job 8:6–8; 11:2–4; 22:21–30). They accused him over and over to try to get him to confess. Finally, Job said, "Miserable comforters are you all!" (Job 16:2, NIV). Rather than comforting Job, they increased his pain.

Section 5.   15 min

How can we help each other grieve?

DISCUSSION

F | *(5 min) Small group or pairs. Mention the section title, then divide the questions among the groups.*

1. When you have been grieving the loss of someone or something, what sort of helpful things have people done or said? What sort of unhelpful things have been done or said?
2. How does your culture traditionally help those who grieve? What customs are helpful? Which ones are not helpful? Which traditions are in keeping with Scripture?

F | *(10 min) Large group. Get feedback. If you are using a board or flip chart, list "helpful" and "unhelpful" things in two columns. Add content below that was not mentioned.*

Here are some ways we can help each other grieve:

A. Emotional Help
- Visit the grieving person, when appropriate.
- When they are ready, encourage them to talk about how they feel. Allow them to express their anger and sadness.
- Listen to their pain. Do more listening than talking. They cannot absorb teaching and preaching at this time (Job 21:2; Proverbs 18:13).
- Help them to understand that it is normal to grieve, and that it is a process that will take time. They will not always feel like they do right now. It is important that they do not make

major changes based on how they feel as they go through Neighborhood 1 and 2. When they are in Neighborhood 3, they will be able to make better decisions.

- When people are ready, you can pray with or for them (Ephesians 6:18). You can also read a promise from the Bible and encourage them to memorize it. For example: "The LORD is near to those who are discouraged; he saves those who have lost all hope" (Psalm 34:18).

- Eventually, they need to bring their pain to God. The more specific they can be about their loss, the better. For example, they may have lost a loved one, but also an income, companionship, respect, or security. They should bring these losses to God one by one.

B. Practical Help

If a grieving person has to worry about caring for themselves and their family, they will not have enough energy to grieve properly and recover. They might be too exhausted to do the work they did before, much less to do all the things the deceased person did.

- Relieve them of their regular responsibilities so that they can grieve. Especially at the time of the funeral and burial, there are many practical ways to help a grieving person. Widows and orphans are in particular need of help, and we are instructed to care for them (James 1:27).

- If there is no corpse, arrange a service to remember the person's life and to publicly acknowledge their death. A photo of the person can take the place of the corpse. If the family is dispersed, those who are displaced or grieving from a distance can hold similar ceremonies.

- It is not unusual for a person to have difficulty sleeping in the early weeks and months after a loss. If people are not able to sleep, encourage them to get physical exercise. As appropriate, encourage them to take walks, do outdoor work, or get involved in sports. Getting exhausted will help them sleep better at night.

- If the person denies that their loved one has died, gently help them realize it in small ways. For example, help the person to disperse their loved one's personal belongings.

F *Take a short break before beginning the lament section.*

Laments   40–55 min

F *(10 min) Present the content below. Bring out that the only part that must be present in a lament is the complaint.*

In Psalm 13:1, David asks, "How much longer will you forget me, Lord? Forever?" In verse 6, he says, "I will sing to you, O Lord, because you have been good to me." How can David say both of these things at the same time? They seem contradictory.

God has given us a tool to help us express our grief. It is called a lament. Many of the psalms are laments. In a lament, people pour out their complaints to God in an effort to persuade him to act on their behalf, all the while stating their trust in him (Psalm 62:8). A lament can be composed by an individual or by a community.

Laments can have seven parts:

- Address to God ("O God")
- Review of God's faithfulness in the past
- **A complaint**
- A confession of sin or claim of innocence
- A request for help
- God's response (often not stated)
- A vow to praise, statement of trust in God

Not all parts are present in each lament, and they are not always in the same order. But there is always a complaint.

Laments allow a person to fully express their grief, and even accuse God. This is often, but not always, followed by a statement of trust in God (see Psalm 88 and Lamentations). This combination makes for very powerful prayers. The grief is not hidden, but rather expressed openly to God. Laments encourage people to be honest with God, to speak the truth about their feelings and doubts. To lament to God is a sign of faith, not of doubt.

In a lament, people do not attempt to solve the problem themselves, but they cry to God for help. They look to God, not the enemy, as the one ultimately in control of the situation. They ask God to take action to bring justice rather than taking action themselves (Psalm 28:3–4).

Laments are well known in many communities. They are a good way to express deep emotions.

EXERCISE

F | *(5 min) Read Psalm 13 (below) out loud as a group and identify the parts of the lament (vs. 1–2, address and complaint; vs. 3–4, request; vs. 5a, statement of trust in God; vs. 5b–6, vow to praise). Then read the lament instructions in number 2.*

1. Can you identify the parts of this lament?
   Psalm 13

   1 *How much longer will you forget me, LORD? Forever?*
      How much longer will you hide yourself from me?

   2 *How long must I endure trouble?*
      How long will sorrow fill my heart day and night?
      How long will my enemies triumph over me?

   3 *Look at me, O LORD my God, and answer me.*
      Restore my strength; don't let me die.

   4 *Don't let my enemies say, "We have defeated him."*
      Don't let them gloat over my downfall.

   5 *I rely on your constant love;*
      I will be glad, because you will rescue me.

   6 *I will sing to you, O LORD,*
      because you have been good to me.

2. Take some time to create a lament to God. Your lament could be a song, rap, poem, prayer, dance, or any creative way you wish to express your feelings to God. It does not have to include all parts of a lament, but it does need to have a complaint.

F (20–30 min) Lament Exercise. It is best to let people work in silence, without background music, as the music can be distracting. Have participants maintain silence until you bring the group back.

If participants have experienced a traumatic event as a community, it may be beneficial to create a lament as a group. This will often be creating a song to sing together. Have them work in small groups or one large group. To start the process, have participants identify the theme of their lament. Have them explore their feelings and the questions they have for God about the situation.

DISCUSSION

F (5–10 min) Small group or pairs.

Share as much or as little as you would like of your lament. Or, if you would prefer, share what the process of writing a lament was like for you.

Closing   5 min

F (5 min) Give time for one or more participants to share their lament with the large group. You may also want to sing a song of lament together or choose a lament psalm to read out loud as a closing prayer. Then give them time to reflect on the Closing question. Encourage the participants to read the lesson and look up the Scripture passages after the session.

What is one thing you want to remember from this lesson?

F If desired, after this lesson and before the next, you may insert one or more of the following optional lessons:
  • How can we help children who have experienced bad things?
  • Rape and other forms of sexual assault
  • HIV and AIDS
  • Domestic abuse
  • Suicide
  • Addictions
  • Caring for the caregiver

5. Bringing our pain to the cross

Before you begin:

- Well before this lesson, read "Note to facilitator" below and discuss the details with the host, to ensure you will be doing the lesson in the most culturally appropriate way.
- Identify one or more participants who can assist you with the lesson and review it with them at least a full day before the lesson.
- Schedule a break at the end of this lesson, so that people have time to reflect on the experience.
- Prepare materials (see list below).
- Arrange the chairs in the most appropriate way for the ceremony (such as a circle or other formation that is different than a classroom style).
- For Section 1: Decide how you will present the story (page 190, "Stories" in "Preparing the lessons").
- For Sections 2 & 3: Select the songs and instrumental music you will use.

In this lesson we will:

- Identify our heart wounds and share them with another person.
- Discuss how Jesus died to heal our wounds as well as forgive our sins.
- Bring our pain to the cross of Jesus and help others do the same.

Section 1: Story	15 min
Section 2: Identify the wounds of your heart	50 min
Section 3: Bring your pain to Jesus	25 min
Total time	**1 hour 30 minutes**

NOTE TO FACILITATOR:
This exercise should be done toward the end of the healing group, after people have been thinking about their heart wounds and feel ready to bring their pain to God. Do it in a way that people know that what they write will never be seen by others. The exercise is not a magic ritual but is a way for us to experience God beginning to heal our pain.

Details to discuss with the host in advance:
- Does a church leader need to help lead this lesson? If yes, who?
- Can a cross be used? If so, are there any concerns about the kind of cross? Can papers be nailed to the cross? If not, can they be taped to it, or placed in a box at the foot of the cross?
- Can the cross be carried?
- Would it be more appropriate to refer to this lesson with your groups as "Bringing our pain to Jesus"?

- Are there any security concerns about people writing down their pain?
- What is the best way to group participants during the sharing time in Section 2? (see "Other considerations," below)

Other considerations:

- If you know that one or more of the participants experienced a traumatic event that included fire, consider using one of the methods listed below for destroying the papers that does not use fire. Or if the event included water, consider not using water in the ceremony.

- Decide how best to group participants during Section 2, when the large group is divided into small groups of two or three and each person has the opportunity to share their deepest pain. Sometimes, it is important to keep men with men, pastors with pastors, and women with women. If one goal of the healing group is ethnic reconciliation, people from different ethnic groups could be put together. When people trust each other enough to share and hear each other's deepest pain, healing often takes place. Encourage participants to find someone they would like to share with. Be careful no one is left without a partner, unless by choice.

- It may be good to talk about the experience the next time your group meets, to discuss how people felt about it and how they are feeling now.

- If you did the Moral injury lesson with your group, consider modifying the Pain to the Cross lesson as follows:

  - Add a pitcher of water, a bowl, and hand towel on a small stand a short distance from the cross.

  - In Section 2, during "Time alone," modify the instructions of the first paragraph as indicated by the following bold text: *Take some time alone and reflect on the pain(s) you want to bring to Jesus for healing. Write on paper the things that give you pain—things done to you,* **and things you have done, left undone, or witnessed that may have created a wound for you.** *Or you can draw a picture if you would like or create some other expression of the pain you would like to process.*

  - In Section 3, when you invite the participants to bring their pain to the cross, invite them also to then take a moment to wash their hands with the pitcher of water (or have a person hold the pitcher and pour water onto the outstretched hands of each participant). Remind participants that this is not a "magic cleansing" from their soul wound but a symbolic reminder of the washing away of sin and receiving God's forgiveness.

Materials to prepare in advance:

A cross, such as:

- a wooden cross, if the papers will be nailed to the cross.
- any other type of cross, if the papers will not be nailed to the cross.
- a cross drawn on a box.
- if the symbol of the cross is not acceptable to the group, use a plain box for participants to put their papers in.
- if it is not appropriate to use a cross, discuss with the host what would be the best way to do this ceremony.

A pen and paper for each person:

- Some facilitators prefer to give each participant many small papers and have them write one pain per paper.
- Some facilitators prefer using dissolving paper.
- If paper is not available or if people are not literate, or if they are afraid their security might be at risk if they write down their pain, have them represent each pain with an object that can be burned—for example, a small stick or a drawing on a paper.

A method to destroy to the papers, such as:
- burning them: matches, a container in which to burn the papers, a stick or other tool to stir the fire, a place outside to burn them.
- dissolving them: dissolving paper, a bucket of water, and a stick or other tool to stir the water.
- shredding them: a paper shredder, or ask the participants to tear them up into tiny pieces.
- blotting them out: black paint to pour over the papers, and a bowl or tray in which to place the papers.
- any creative method of destroying the papers.

Nails and a hammer if the papers are to be nailed to the cross, or tape if they are to be attached to the cross, or a basket if the papers are laid at the foot of the cross.

Song sheets or recorded music. Choose songs that most, if not all, people know; this is not the time to teach new songs,

5. Bringing our pain to the cross

F | *(1 min) Introduce lesson title and objectives. Direct participants to the corresponding lesson in Healing the Wounds of Trauma. Briefly explain the Pain to the Cross ceremony, so participants will know what to expect.*

Section 1.

15 min

Jesus sets a woman free

F | *(3 min) Large group. Present the story.*

Jesus had been asked to go and heal a young girl who was very ill. As he was on his way, there were people following and crowding around him. A woman in the crowd had suffered for twelve years with constant bleeding. She had suffered a great deal from many doctors, and over the years she had spent everything she had to pay them, but she had gotten no better. In fact, she had gotten worse. She had heard about Jesus, so she came up behind him through the crowd and touched his robe. For she thought to herself, "If I can just touch his robe, I will be healed." Immediately the bleeding stopped, and she could feel in her body that she had been healed of her terrible condition.

Jesus realized at once that healing power had gone out from him, so he turned around in the crowd and asked, "Who touched my robe?"

His disciples said to him, "Look at this crowd pressing around you. How can you ask, 'Who touched me?'"

But he kept on looking around to see who had done it. Then the frightened woman, trembling at the realization of what had happened to her, came and fell to her knees in front of him. The whole crowd heard her explain why she had touched him and that she had been immediately healed. Jesus said to her, "Daughter, your faith has made you well. Go in peace. Your suffering is over." (Adapted from Mark 5:25–34 NLT)

DISCUSSION

F | *(12 min) Large group, except for Questions 5 and 6.*

1. How would you describe this woman?
2. What happened when she touched Jesus?
3. Why do you think Jesus did not just let her disappear into the crowd?
4. How did she think Jesus would respond to her when she told the whole truth of her story? How did he respond?

In groups of two or three:

5. Have you ever felt ashamed of your story?

6. How do you think Jesus would respond if you told him the whole truth of your story?

F | *If the participants are using books, encourage them to keep them closed for the rest of the lesson.*

Section 2.   50 min

Identify the wounds of your heart

F | *(5 min) Begin with a song, then present the content below.*

Just as the person in the story took their pain to Jesus, we can do the same.

We are taught in Scripture that Jesus came not only to bear our sins but also to bear our pain and heal us. The Gospel of Matthew quotes the prophet Isaiah to describe what Jesus did: "He took our sickness and carried away our diseases" (Matthew 8:17, quoting Isaiah 53:4). In the same passage from the prophet Isaiah, it also says:

> *He was despised and rejected by mankind,*
> *a man of suffering, and familiar with pain.*
> *Like one from whom people hide their faces*
> *he was despised, and we held him in low esteem.*
> *But he was pierced for our transgressions,*
> *he was crushed for our iniquities;*
> *the punishment that brought us peace was on him,*
> *and by his wounds we are healed. (Isaiah 53:3, 5 NIV)*

Jesus felt the full burden of human pain and sinfulness. Jesus knows the pain that is in our hearts and we need to bring it to him so he can heal us.

TIME ALONE

F | *(20 min) Present the paper(s). Present the paragraphs below. Tell participants how much time they will have alone and how you will call them back (for example, by your voice or a bell or by playing instrumental music). It is preferable to do this part in silence.*

Now we would like you to take some time alone and reflect on the pain(s) you want to bring to Jesus for healing. Write on the paper we have given you the things that give you pain–things done to you or things that you have done. If you prefer, you can draw a picture or create some other way of expressing the pain. Please feel free now to find a quiet place alone, and we will call you back to this place afterward.

F | *(5 min) When time is up, call participants back. Sing a song together.*

DISCUSSION

F | *(20 min) Groups of two or three. Tell participants how many minutes they will have or that they should come back when they hear the bell or music.*

We will now give you an opportunity to share these pains with another person, if you would like. You may share as much or as little as you would like of what you have put on your paper. Or you may share what the experience was like of writing it. After sharing, take time to pray for each other. If you are not comfortable sharing what is in your heart, it's okay; you can simply pray together.

F | *When time is up, call participants back, with your voice or the bell or by singing a chorus.*

Section 3.

25 min

Bring your pain to Jesus

F | *(1 min) Read the paragraph below out loud. Modify the instructions as needed if you are using dissolving paper, or if the host has approved the option of having participants nail their pain to the cross.*

Jesus said, "Come to me, all of you who are tired from carrying heavy loads, and I will give you rest. Take my yoke and put it on you, and learn from me, because I am gentle and humble in spirit; and you will find rest" (Matthew 11:28–29). Jesus invites you to come to him. When you are ready, you can bring your papers to the cross. If you would like, you can say, "I am bringing my pain to Jesus." Feel free to linger at the cross as long as you need. If you are not ready to bring your paper to the cross, feel free to stay where you are.

TIME TO BRING OUR PAIN TO JESUS

F | *(10 min) Invite participants to bring their pain to the cross. If desired, sing a song together. Then take the papers outside (in procession with the cross, if appropriate) and burn them, while reading the content below. If desired, read Revelation 21:1-5 in addition to Isaiah 61:1-4 (footnote).*

Revelation 21:1-5

Then I saw a new heaven and a new earth. The first heaven and the first earth disappeared, and the sea vanished. And I saw the Holy City, the new Jerusalem, coming down out of heaven from God, prepared and ready, like a bride dressed to meet her husband. I heard a loud voice speaking from the throne: "Now God's home is with people! He will live with them, and they shall be his people. God himself will be with them, and he will be their God. He will wipe away all tears from their eyes. There will be no more death, no more grief or crying or pain. The old things have disappeared." Then the one who sits on the throne said, "And now I make all things new!" He also said to me, "Write this, because these words are true and can be trusted."

By destroying our papers, we are asking Jesus to take our suffering and continue to lead us on a journey of healing. This is not magic. It is something we do with our whole body that helps our heart and mind understand that we are asking Jesus to take our pain.

In Luke 4, Jesus himself read part of the following passage and helped people understand that it refers to himself.

Isaiah 61:1–4 says:

> *The Sovereign LORD has filled me with his Spirit.*
> *He has chosen me and sent me*
> *To bring good news to the poor,*
> *To heal the broken-hearted,*
> *To announce release to captives*
> *And freedom to those in prison.*
> *He has sent me to proclaim*
> *That the time has come*
> *When the LORD will save his people*
> *And defeat their enemies.*
> *He has sent me to comfort all who mourn,*
> *To give to those who mourn in Zion*
> *Joy and gladness instead of grief,*
> *A song of praise instead of sorrow.*
> *They will be like trees*
> *That the LORD himself has planted.*
> *They will all do what is right,*
> *And God will be praised for what he has done.*
> *They will rebuild cities that have long been in ruins.*

SHARE

F | *(10 min) Ask the question below and allow time for some participants to share.*

Is there anything you want to share about what God has done for you during our time together?

F | *(4 min) As you close, tell participants that it is normal to feel more tired or emotional than usual after this lesson, because they have let deep emotions out. This is part of healing. Encourage them to take care good of themselves, and to contact the facilitators if they need extra support.*
Pray for the participants. Sing an appropriate song together. Dismiss.

6. How can we forgive others?

If this will be the last lesson of your healing group, decide if you will use the "Looking back and looking forward" section (page 68) and which closing activities you will use (Closing section).

Before you begin:

- For Section 1: Decide if you will use the story or the skits. If people in your group have experienced domestic abuse issues and you are using the story instead of the skits, it is important to go through the domestic abuse optional lesson before doing the forgiveness lesson. If using the skits, arrange in advance for eight participants to act out them out. If needed, make copies of the skits for them. If using the story, decide how you will present it (see page <?>, "Stories" in "Preparing the lessons").
- For Section 3: Familiarize yourself with the cell phone skit.
- For Section 3: Draw the forgiveness cycle on the board, flip chart, or large paper.
- For Section 4: Familiarize yourself with the rope skit or one of the supplemental skits. Get a rope or something you can use to tie two people together.
- For Sections 3, 4, and 5B: If needed, prepare slips of paper or index cards with Bible verses or use the Bible verses download.

In this lesson we will:

- Discuss what forgiveness is and is not.
- Explain how to forgive others—the process.
- Explain why we need to forgive others, especially as Christians.
- Explain the process of true repentance.
- Identify those we need to forgive or ask forgiveness from.

Section 1: Story or skits	10 min
Section 2: What is forgiveness and what is it not?	15 min
Section 3: How can we forgive others?	43 min
Section 4: Why should we forgive other people?	32 min
Section 5: What if we are the ones who have caused the offense?	15 min
Closing	5 min
Total time	**2 hours**

6. How can we forgive others?

F | *(1 min) Introduce lesson title and objectives. Direct participants to the corresponding lesson in Healing the Wounds of Trauma.*

Section 1. A forgiveness story or skits   10 min

A. Ann forgives Joe

F | *(5 min) Large group. Present the story.*

Ann had been living separately from Joe for one year. Her heart was bitter because Joe had treated her cruelly and beaten her and their son. Meanwhile, Joe was feeling lonely. He felt guilty for hurting Ann. He also felt deep remorse that he had ruined his family. Joe wanted to change and become a better person. So, throughout the past year, Joe had been meeting with Pastor Mark regularly for counseling.

One day one of Ann's friends told her, "Ann, you need to forgive your husband now for what he did and forget all those things in the past." Ann did not have the energy to explain how confused she felt, so she said quickly, "I've forgiven Joe. I don't remember what he did anymore." But in her heart, Ann could not forget what he had done.

One day Ann heard Pastor Mark preach a sermon in church about how Jesus told Peter to forgive an offender seventy times seven times. She wondered how that applied to her feelings about Joe. She no longer wanted to harm him, but she did not know how to forgive him or whether that would mean she would need to return to him.

That night she went to meet with her friend, Hannah, Pastor Mark's wife. Ann told her that she had tried to forgive Joe and forget what he had done. There was a pause, and then Ann admitted, "But I have not been able to forget what he did, and it makes me feel horrible."

Hannah asked her, "Who told you that you must forget? You will always remember what happened, but each time you remember, you can take the pain to Jesus and forgive again. Little by little you will remember what happened without feeling as much of the pain."

Ann went home and began to ask God to help her truly forgive Joe. Gradually she began to let go of her anger and hurt. Sometimes she would remember the horrible things he had done, and she would have to ask God to help her forgive Joe again. Over time the anger in her heart began to go away and she began to feel God's peace.

DISCUSSION

F | *(5 min) Large group.*

1. Why did Ann have trouble forgiving Joe?
2. What do you think about how Hannah explained forgiveness to Ann?

F | *If the participants are using books, encourage them to keep them closed for the rest of the lesson.*

B. Forgiveness skits

SKIT 1

(Caleb is talking with his friend Tim.)

Caleb: You know, Tim, last week Simon really hurt me. Right in front of all the other pastors he said I was no good at preaching sermons. I can't get over it. It still hurts when I think about it.

(Tim leaves and Simon walks in)

Simon: Hey, Caleb, please forgive me for what I said last week about you being no good at preaching. I shouldn't have said that.

Caleb: Oh, don't worry about that. There's nothing to forgive. I didn't mind.

SKIT 2

(James is talking to Adam, a good friend.)

James: Hey, Adam, you seem upset. What's up?

Adam: I've tried to forgive my father for being cruel to me when I was a child, but it is hard.

James: Well, you must forget all about that. Until you forget, you can't say you have forgiven him.

SKIT 3

Ruth: Hey, thanks for teaching the class last week for me, Anna.

Anna: I never want to teach that class again! I was trying to talk about Laments in the Psalms, and Sarah kept saying how we shouldn't say the word "Selah." And she just wouldn't let it go. I felt very embarrassed and disrespected.

Ruth: Well, have you been able to talk with Sarah?

Anna: No, I haven't.

Ruth: Would you like me to go with you to talk with her?

Anna: Would you? That would be great!

(Ruth and Anna go and knock on Sarah's door.)

Sarah: Hi, ladies! Come on in. Would you like a cup of tea? Hey, Anna, I was just thinking about you. I am soooo sorry about how I kept disrupting Bible class last week. You were doing a good job filling in for Ruth, and I'm pretty sure I was obsessing on the phrase "Selah" and its importance. It was arrogant and insensitive of me. I'm so sorry. Could you please forgive me?

Anna: Thanks, Sarah. I appreciate that. I was embarrassed by your interruptions and felt like you didn't respect me much. I see now you didn't mean to be that way. Yes, of course, I forgive you.

Sarah: Oh, thank you, Anna. I so appreciate your honesty and your forgiveness. Do you have time to stay for tea?

DISCUSSION

F | *(5 min) Large group.*

Which of these situations shows real forgiveness? How is it different from the others?

F | *If the participants are using books, encourage them to keep them closed for the rest of the lesson.*

Section 2.

15 min

What is forgiveness and what is it not?

DISCUSSION

F | *(5 min) Large group. Discuss the question below.*

1. What are some common sayings about forgiveness in your culture?

F | *(5 min) Small group. Ask the question below, then divide the statements below among the small groups or pairs to discuss.*

2. Do you think the following statements about forgiveness are true or false? Why?
    a. Forgiveness is saying the offense didn't matter or that we were not hurt by what the person did.
    b. Forgiveness is a process that may take time.
    c. Forgiveness is acting as if the event never happened.
    d. Forgiveness is understanding why the person did what he or she did.
    e. Forgiveness is not dependent on the offender apologizing first or changing his or her behavior.
    f. Forgiveness means that we will forget what happened.
    g. Forgiveness is not the same thing as reconciliation.
    h. Forgiveness means that I will completely trust the person I have forgiven.
    i. Forgiveness means that there will be no consequences for the action.
    j. Forgiveness does not mean letting the offender hurt us or other innocent people again.

F | *(5 min) Large group. Get feedback and review the answers to the questions.*

    a. F
    b. T
    c. F
    d. F
    e. T
    f. F
    g. T
    h. F

i. F

j. T

Section 3.

How can we forgive others?

F | *(1 min) Mention the section title. Present the paragraph below.*

6

If we think forgiving is too hard for us to do, we are right. But God can give us the strength to do all things (Philippians 4:13).

DISCUSSION

F | *(5 min) Small group. Assign Q. 1 below to half of the group and Q. 2 to the other half to discuss.*

1. In our last lesson we took our pain to Jesus. How could bringing your pain to Jesus help you forgive?

2. Read Acts 7:59-60 and Romans 12:17-19. How do we forgive, if someone has not asked for forgiveness?

F | *(8 min) Large group. Get feedback, then add content from A. and B. below that was not mentioned.*

A. Be honest about the pain and bring it to Jesus

Forgiving someone means that we recognize that the person has wronged us, and we accept the pain their sin has caused us. We do not minimize the pain but, like the psalmist, we are honest with God about what we are feeling (Psalm 6:2–3, 6–7).

Our pain may last a long time, but we continue to bring it to Jesus, who understands the pain of being wronged by others (Luke 18:31–33; Isaiah 53:3). As Jesus heals us, then we will be able to forgive those who have hurt us.

B. Release the offender to God without waiting for them to apologize

Often, we are unwilling to forgive until the offender has apologized to us. Or we want to see that the person has changed their behavior before we forgive them. However, Jesus and Stephen asked God to forgive the people who were killing them (Luke 23:34; Acts 7:59-60).

When we forgive, we release the offender and our wish for their harm to God. Instead of paying the person back, we put them into God's hands (Romans 12:17–19). We let go of our own right to judge and allow God to do so, knowing that he will judge with justice and righteousness (Psalm 9:8).

C. Allow time for the process

F | *(5 min) Large group. Present the following paragraph, then ask a volunteer to act out the skit as you read it aloud.*

Forgiveness does not happen all at once. We decide to forgive, but sometimes as we remember the offense, we go back to feeling bitter. When this happens, we need to continue to take the pain to Jesus and reaffirm our commitment to forgive again.

CELL PHONE SKIT

Robbers took Elizabeth's money and phone and damaged a lot of her things. She spent some time in the Neighborhood of Denial and Anger. Then she prayed: "God, I know you want me to forgive the robbers; please help me." Take five steps forward.

Then she has to stand in line for three hours to get a replacement cell phone. She feels very angry at the robbers—take three steps back. She prays again for God to help her forgive. Take five steps forward.

Then her child comes to her and needs money for school supplies—and she does not have it. She feels more anger at the robbers—three steps back. She prays again for God to help her forgive. Five steps forward.

Two months later is Christmas and she does not have the money for the gifts and special food that she usually does every year. She feels the anger—three steps back—and prays for God to help her forgive—five steps forward.

On the anniversary of the robbery she is able to pray to God without feeling the old anger.

F | (5 min) Ask the participants, "What did you see?" and discuss the skit.
(3 min) Draw the forgiveness cycle on the board, flip chart, or large paper, and present the description below it. See footnote for an optional diagram.

Fig. 6.1: The cycle of forgiveness

The 'cage'
of the offense

Optional forgiveness diagram

Fig. 6.1.B: The cycle of forgiveness

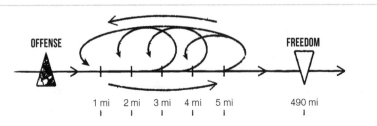

The commitment to forgive often comes before we experience any feelings of forgiveness—sometimes long before. Like the bird in the diagram, we may circle back many times in our hearts toward the "cage" of the offense. As we forgive again and again, eventually we will feel less pain when we remember the event. Just like the bird flies higher and farther from the cage, toward freedom, we move increasingly toward freedom each time we renew our commitment to forgive.

D. Let the offender face the consequences of their actions

DISCUSSION

F | *(10 min) Large group. Discuss, then add the content below that was not mentioned.*

Read Romans 13:1-4 and Numbers 5:5-7. What is the relationship between forgiveness and consequences?

Forgiving someone does not mean that they should not be punished if they have done wrong things. Even though we have forgiven someone, it may be necessary to bring them to justice to prevent them from hurting others in the future and to give them the opportunity to repent.

God has given national and traditional leaders the job of punishing criminals and protecting the innocent (Romans 13:1–4). God has charged church leaders to protect the innocent, too. They should never ignore or cover up sin but need to address it honestly (Proverbs 18:5; Ephesians 5:11; Galatians 6:1).

Forgiveness does not mean that the offender is excused from paying back what was taken. Some things can never be repaid. But if someone has stolen something, for example, the thief should return or replace it (Numbers 5:5–7; Philemon 18–19).

E. Determine if and when you are able to trust the offender again

DISCUSSION

F | *(5 min) Large group. Discuss, then add content below that was not mentioned.*

What signs did Joseph see in his brothers that indicated they could be trusted again? (Consider Genesis 42:21 and 44:30-34)

If we forgive someone, it does not mean that we trust him or her immediately. Just because we have forgiven a person does not mean that he or she has changed. Even if there is a change, trust has been broken and will take time to rebuild. Little by little, if we have good experiences with that person, we can begin to trust him or her again. But it may take a long time before we can trust him or her completely. In some cases, it may never be safe to trust the person again.

Before trusting his brothers, Joseph put them through some tests when they came to Egypt, to see whether they had changed (Genesis 42–44).

Forgiveness can open the way for our relationship with a person to be restored. It may cause the offender to repent and reconcile. But they may not choose to be reconciled to us. Even if we want a relationship to be restored, it requires action by both parties. Reconciliation is not always appropriate, for example, in certain cases of abuse.

Conclusion

F | *(1 min) Present the following paragraph.*

Forgiveness is a decision to release our right to pay back the offender. It acknowledges what has happened and how it has affected us. It is an ongoing process of reaffirming our decision to let go each time we remember the offense. It does not require us to trust the person again nor release them from the consequences of the offense.

Section 4.

32 min

Why should we forgive other people?

F | *(5 min) Mention the section title. Do the rope skit (below) or one of the supplemental skits (footnote) to illustrate why we should forgive.*

Rope skit

Get two volunteers of the same gender. Tie the two volunteers together back to back with a rope or long cloth. (If preferred, have them lock elbows.) Then read the skit below, while the volunteers act out your instructions.

Sam (or Samantha) was offended by his (or her) friend. Everywhere Sam goes, he drags his friend with him like a lot of extra weight. This is exhausting and frustrating for him.

- *When Sam takes a walk, his friend is there.*
- *When Sam eats supper, his friend is there.*
- *When Sam tries to do his work, his friend is there.*
- *When Sam prays, his friend is there.*
- *When Sam tries to run away, his friend follows.*
- *When Sam tries to hide, his friend is right there.*

Supplemental rope skit

Use a very long rope, cloth, or cord. Get volunteers to play the part of each person mentioned:

Say, "John (or Joanna) won't forgive his mother for something she did in his childhood." (Hand one end of the rope to John. Have the mother take hold of the rope.) "He has carried her around since childhood." (Have John and the mother take a few steps together.)

Say, "John had an argument with his boss last month and even though the boss said sorry, John will not forgive him—so he joins the mother." (Have the boss take hold of the rope. Have them all take a few steps together.)

Add others until John is pulling around a large group of people.

Ask, "How does John feel? What do you think he should do?" (When participants say, "He needs to forgive," have him let go of the rope.)

Discuss the effects of having a habit of not forgiving others.

Supplemental cloth skit

Have two participants hold opposite ends of a towel or other piece of cloth, or a thick rope. Describe a situation in which one of the participants is the offender and the other is the one who needs to forgive. Have the participants twist the ends in opposite directions so that the towel tightens and knots in the middle. Present this as a picture of not forgiving and its results: tension, knots in the stomach, and so forth.

Ask, "What must be done to get rid of the knots?" (One person, at least, has to let go of their end of the dispute, argument, or desire for revenge. If the other person also lets go, reconciliation can happen.) Have the person on one end let go of his or her end.

Say, "The Bible tells us, 'Dear friends, don't try to get even. Let God take revenge. In the Scriptures the Lord says, "I am the one to take revenge and pay them back"'" (Romans 12:19 CEV). We need to choose to let go of our unforgiveness and leave the person that has hurt us in God's hands. Then we move forward in the plans God has for us."

No matter where Sam goes, he cannot escape his thoughts and feelings about his friend. He cannot escape them until he forgives.

    (Have Sam then forgive his friend, and as he does, release the rope.)

Carrying the bitterness is like having the offender attached to us and taking them with us wherever we go. Forgiveness is a gift that we have received from God, and one that we should also pass along to others (Matthew 18:21–35).

DISCUSSION

F   *(5 min) Small group. Divide the verses among the groups.*

What do the following verses say about why we should forgive?

Ephesians 4:26–27	2 Corinthians 2:10–11	Hebrews 12:14–15
Matthew 6:12	Ephesians 4:32	Matthew 18:21–35

F   *(12 min) Large group. Get feedback. Then add content below that was not mentioned.*

A. Forgiveness frees us from anger and bitterness.

It is appropriate for us to feel angry when we have been sinned against. But if we let our anger lead us to sin or if we let it fester, we can give Satan a foothold in our hearts (Ephesians 4:26–27; 2 Corinthians 2:10–11). We become slaves of anger and bitterness and they begin to destroy us. If we do not forgive someone who has offended us, we are the ones who suffer. Refusing to forgive can make us physically ill with headaches, stomach ulcers, or heart problems. It may make us become as violent and evil as those who offended us. Forgiveness releases us from all this.

If we do not forgive others, we can pass our bitterness on to our children. This poison will result in cycles of revenge and violence between groups which can go on for generations (Hebrews 12:14–15). Only forgiveness can break this cycle of revenge.

Fig. 6.2: Forgiveness sets us free

B. Forgiveness shows that we understand how much God has forgiven us.

When we understand how much we owe God because of our sins (Matthew 18:21–35), and how he has forgiven our debt through Jesus (Ephesians 4:32), we will want to extend that same forgiveness to others. But if we refuse to forgive others, it shows we do not understand how much we owed God and how much he has forgiven us (Matthew 6:12).

DISCUSSION

> F | *(10 min) Pairs or small groups. Choose one set of questions. If you choose the first set, get feedback.*

1. What traditions do you have that help you to forgive others? What traditions do you have that hinder you from forgiving?
2. What do you find the hardest thing about forgiving someone? What has helped you the most to forgive others?

Section 5.   15 min

What if we are the ones who have caused the offense?

> F | *(5 min) Mention the section title, then ask, "How can we repent?" Discuss, then add content below that was not mentioned.*

A. How can we repent?

- We allow God's Spirit to show us how much our sin hurts him and others. This may make us sad and even weep (James 4:8–9). This sorrow can be good for us. "For the kind of sorrow God wants us to experience leads us away from sin and results in salvation. There's no regret for that kind of sorrow. But worldly sorrow, which lacks repentance, results in spiritual death" (2 Corinthians 7:10 NLT). Both Peter and Judas were sad that they had denied Jesus, but Peter's sorrow brought him closer to God; Judas's led him to kill himself.
- We take responsibility for what we have done and clearly state our sin (Proverbs 28:13; Psalm 32:3–5).
- We are willing to listen to the person we have hurt express the pain we have caused.
- We seek God's forgiveness of our sin, and then accept that he has done so (1 John 1:9).
- We ask those we have offended to forgive us, without defending ourselves, blaming them, or demanding that they trust us again right away (James 5:16). We should ask forgiveness in such a way that all those affected by our sin are aware of our repentance. For example, if we insulted someone in front of others, then we should ask forgiveness in front of the other people as well.
- If we have repented in our hearts, we will show it by the way we act (Acts 26:20b).
- Repentance may involve paying back what was taken (Numbers 5:5–7).

B. How can we forgive ourselves?

DISCUSSION

> F (10 min) Large group. Discuss, then have participants read 1 John 1:9 and Psalm 103:2-3, 12. Add content below that was not mentioned.

Some people continue to feel guilt, shame, and regret even after doing all they should to repent and make restoration. Why do you think this is?

If our feelings make it seem that God is far away, we can talk to God about this. We can ask him to help us experience the truth that he has forgiven us and has removed our sins from us as far as the east is from the west (1 John 1:9; Psalm 103:2–3, 12). Sometimes we will need other people to help us with this process, like a pastor, a counselor, or a trusted friend. If we are part of a church that shows us love and forgives us, that can help us experience the way God forgives us. This process can take time and the roots of our struggle can be deep. Gradually, our feelings can change to match the truth that we know in our head.

Closing   5 min

> F (5 min) Give participants time to reflect on Question 1. At the end of that time, read 1 John 1:9 aloud together. Then give them time to reflect on Question 2. Encourage the participants to read the lesson and look up the Scripture passages after the session.

1. Ask God to show you any sins of which you need to repent and any people you need to forgive. Confess the sins to God and receive his forgiveness. Ask God to help you forgive the people.

   If we confess our sins to God, he will keep his promise and do what is right: he will forgive us our sins and purify us from all our wrongdoing. (1 John 1:9)

2. What is one thing you want to remember from this lesson?

> F If desired, after this lesson and before the next, you may do the lesson on Preparing for trouble.

Looking back & looking forward

Use this section at the end of the Forgiveness lesson, or at a final gathering, after participants have had some time to reflect on their experience in the healing group.

Before you begin:

- For Section 2: If needed, prepare slips of paper or index cards with Bible verses or use the Bible verses download.
- Plan your Closing activities (Closing section).

In this section we will:

- Illustrate visually the trauma healing journey we have taken and will continue to take.
- Discuss how we have begun to make sense of our faith in God in the midst of suffering.

Section 1: The healing journey	5 min
Section 2: How does God use suffering in people's lives?	20 min
Closing	5 min or more
Total time	**30 minutes**

Looking back & looking forward

F | *(1 min) Mention the section title and objectives.*

Section 1. The healing experience

F | *(4 min) Draw the healing experience diagram and present the content below.*

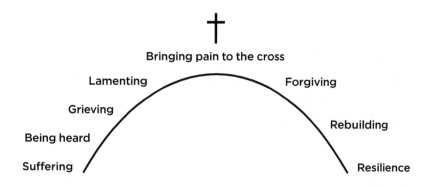

Healing from heart wounds is a process. We have learned several parts of that process—remembering God's love, expressing our pain through words and art, grieving, lamenting, bringing our pain to the cross, and forgiving. When our wounds are deep, we may need to use the things we have learned several times and allow time for God to continue healing our hearts. These are also things we can do when we face new difficulties in our lives. As we practice these things, we will be able to rebuild our lives and be better able to face suffering in the future. This is called resilience. We will have good days and bad days—it is all part of the journey. And as we learned in our time together, we can talk to God at every step.

Section 2.   20 min

How does God use suffering in people's lives?

DISCUSSION IN PAIRS OR SMALL GROUP

F | *(10 min) Pairs or small group. For Question 2, give each group one of the verses.*

1. How has God used suffering in your life?
2. Read the following verses and discuss how God has used suffering in people's lives: 2 Corinthians 1:3–5, Genesis 50:18–20, 1 Peter 1:6–7

F | (10 min) Large group. Get feedback on Question 2. Add content below that was not mentioned, particularly subsection D.

A. God comforts us in our suffering so we can comfort others.

God comforts us when we suffer. He holds us in his arms (Isaiah 40:11). He comforts us with his Word (Psalm 119:50, 92). We can pass on this same comfort to others when they suffer (2 Corinthians 1:3–5).

B. God works so that good comes out of evil.

Joseph's brothers sold him into slavery, but God used this experience to deliver the Israelites from famine (Genesis 50:18–20). God turned the greatest evil that was ever done into the greatest good for us all when Jesus was crucified on the cross (Acts 3:13–15; Philippians 2:8–11). God works in ways we do not always understand, but we can always trust him to bring good ultimately, even if we do not see it in our lifetime (Romans 8:28; 11:33–36).

C. God uses suffering to strengthen our faith.

Suffering strengthens our faith if we let it and increases our ability to endure (Romans 5:3–5; James 1:2–4). Suffering is like fire: it is painful, but it results in purifying our faith in God. When gold is heated over a very hot fire, the bits of dirt in it rise to the top. These can be skimmed off, leaving pure gold (1 Peter 1:6–7).

D. God uses suffering to point us to the new heavens and new earth.

When we suffer, we can think about the eternal kingdom that God is preparing for us (2 Corinthians 4:16–18), when Satan will be defeated (Revelation 20:10) and God will bring an end to evil and suffering (Isaiah 65:17, 25; Revelation 21:1–5).

Closing   5 min or more

F | Here are some ideas for how you can close your healing group:
- *Sing a song together.*
- *Allow time for participants to pray for each other in small groups.*
- *Provide time for participants to exchange contact information and/or to take a group photo, if they desire. Decide together if the group photo can be shared on social media. If necessary, sign the group authorization form (appendix).*
- *Give participants the opportunity to fill out the participant feedback form (appendix).*

What is one thing you want to remember from this lesson?

7. Moral injury

Before you begin:

- For Section 1: Decide which story you will use and how you will present it (see page 190, "Stories" in "Preparing the lessons").
- For Sections 4 and 5: If needed, prepare slips of paper or index cards with Bible verses or download the Bible verses PDF. If your participants are using the Scripture Companion Booklet, you will need to print the discussion verses for these sections, as they are not printed in full in the booklet.
- For the Closing: Decide which exercise you will use and prepare accordingly.

In this lesson we will:

- Describe some of the causes and effects of a moral injury.
- Identify common emotional, spiritual, and behavioral responses to moral injury.
- Give biblical support for how to handle feelings of guilt and shame.
- Identify helpful ways to care for those experiencing moral injury.

Section 1: Story	10 min
Section 2: What is moral injury?	20 min
Section 3: What are the effects of moral injury?	20 min
Section 4: Moral injury in the Bible	20 min
Section 5: How can we help someone with moral injury?	45 min
Closing	5 min
Total time	**2 hours**

7. Moral injury

F (1 min) Introduce lesson title and objectives. Direct participants to the corresponding lesson in Healing the Wounds of Trauma. Choose one of the two following stories, according to the needs of your participants.*

Section 1. Two stories of moral injury

A. Joe's story   (10 min)

F (5 min) Large group. Present the story.

Joe was tense and alert. His special combat unit was patrolling a highly insecure area, and he felt responsible for the safety of his team. Suddenly, they saw a teenage boy approaching from a distance. The boy waved and called out to them.

Joe was in front. He yelled out loudly "Halt! Stop!" and pointed his weapon at the boy. "Stop or we shoot!" Two other soldiers in his unit did the same, but the boy kept walking towards them with something in his hand. Joe felt time stand still. He knew he would have to shoot if the boy took one more step. But he was only a boy! His mind searched desperately for a way out. Again he screamed "Stop!" but the boy took another fateful step. Instinct and training kicked in. Joe discharged his weapon and the boy fell to the ground, dead, a pack of bread rolling from his limp hand.

The scene is still etched in Joe's mind and heart two years later. Joe has never shared the story with anyone, not even his priest. He struggles with guilt and shame. The horror of having taken an innocent life is constantly with him, but he never talks about it. He believes that he is a terrible person and has pulled away from friends and family. He cannot forgive himself and feels that even God cannot forgive him.

His own son, Paul, is thirteen now. Every time Joe looks at Paul, he feels a wave of pain. Even though he loves his son deeply, he finds himself withdrawing from him more and more. Joe doubts that he can be a good father to Paul. He wonders if his son would be better off without him.

DISCUSSION

F (5 min) Large group.

1. What is Joe feeling about himself? About others? About God?
2. What makes it so hard for Joe to recover from this event?

F If the participants are using books, encourage them to keep them closed for the rest of the lesson.

B. Josie's story

F | *(5 min) Large group. Present the story.*

Josie realized she was going to be late picking her daughters up from school. "Not again!" she thought. She grabbed her coat and phone and rushed out of the office. She was waiting for an important response from a client, but there was no way she could be late again. The school had already warned her twice.

Josie pulled the car onto the road and sped up, weaving in and out of traffic. She needed to make up time. This wasn't how she usually drove, but today was an exception. Both girls had soccer games this evening. They would barely have time to get home for a quick dinner before having to race out the door again.

Her phone buzzed. Josie glanced down and saw the incoming text. It was the reply she'd been waiting for. If she did not respond right away, this client might slip away. Josie was a strong advocate against distracted driving. But she knew she was an experienced driver. She could manage this once. She quickly glanced back down and tapped the keyboard.

Josie never saw the bicycle to her right. As she looked down, her car drifted slightly, just enough to hit the bike and send its rider flying. Feeling the bump, Josie slammed on her brakes and pulled over. The car behind her was already stopped, and the driver ran over to the man's body. It was twisted. Josie approached and could immediately see that he was dead. She felt frozen in time. Everything slowed down. Someone pulled her away from the road.

Later, she remembered calling her husband Scott to get their girls. The police came and covered the man's body with a sheet. They took statements from the other drivers. Josie, tears streaming down her face, told the policeman the truth. She explained what a rush she'd been in and how she'd only looked down at her phone for a second.... The officer sadly shook his head.

The next days and weeks were a blur to her. She found herself weeping often and was unable to eat or sleep well. Once she found out that the young man had a wife and baby, Scott and the girls could not console her. Josie no longer wanted to attend church or Bible study. "If they knew what I've done and what a monster I am, they will hate me!" she said. She cannot forgive herself and feels that even God cannot forgive her. Josie told her best friend, Katie, that she felt she could no longer live with herself. Katie went to Scott right away "What should we do, Scott? I am so worried about Josie." Scott felt concerned too. He had never seen Josie like this. She could no longer work, and she avoided time with the family. Her court date was coming up soon, and she did not seem to care what happened to her.

DISCUSSION

F | *(5 min) Large group.*

1. What is Josie feeling about herself? About others? About God?
2. What makes it so hard for Josie to recover from this event?

F | *If the participants are using books, encourage them to keep them closed for the rest of the lesson.*

Section 2.

What is moral injury?

F | *(5 min) Present this content.*

Many people describe moral injury as a type of "soul wound." It happens when people believe they have acted in ways that go against their deepest beliefs about what is right and good, and when others have been harmed as a result. Moral injury may happen when people:

- Feel forced to do something they believe is wrong.
- Are prevented from doing something they believe is right and good.
- Are in situations where there seem to be no good options to prevent harm or make the right choice.
- Realize that they have acted in a way that violates their moral convictions.
- Witness someone doing wrong or not doing right and they do not act to stop it.
- Discover the group they belong to, which they thought was doing good, is actually doing bad things and causing harm.
- Feel they are to blame for others being harmed or dying.

When identifying moral injury, the focus is not on whether the action was sinful. Rather, it is about the impact of the action on the person.

DISCUSSION

F | *(5 min) Small group. Have each group select someone to take notes and speak for the group. (If possible, have the group select a different person for each small group discussion going forward.)*

1. What kinds of events could cause moral injury?
2. Have you known anyone who has suffered in this way?

F | *(10 min) Large group. Get feedback on Question 1. Add content below that was not mentioned.*

Many events can cause moral injury. Common events are when a soldier kills or harms a civilian, a bystander fails to intervene when someone is being harmed, or a person supports an organization or system that ends up harming individuals.

As we learned in Lesson 2, helplessness and horror are often at the center of heart wounds. With a soul wound, the focus tends to be guilt and shame because of something the person did or thinks they did that was deeply wrong. Moral injury needs special care for healing to take place, and even then it may take a long time to heal. Many feel they will never get better.

This diagram illustrates the relationship between moral injury, trauma, and grief. Not all traumatic experiences cause moral injury, and not all moral injury is caused by a traumatic experience. Trauma is caused by something external and is characterized by deep fear. Moral injury comes from inside a person, from the tension between one's beliefs and one's experiences. It is characterized by guilt and especially shame.

Moral injury shows that the person knows what is right and is deeply grieved by wrong. This is a healthier response than being indifferent to wrong.

Fig. 7.1: Moral injury

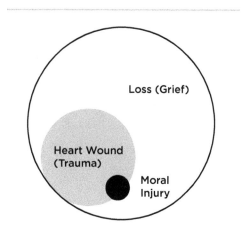

Section 3.

20 min

What are the effects of moral injury?

F | *(1 min) Present the content below.*

People may not be aware they have a moral injury for some time after the event that causes it. Eventually, they begin to experience emotional pain from the deep guilt and shame. Guilt is feeling that we have done something we think is bad. Shame is the feeling that we *are* bad or deeply flawed.

Guilt and shame may be present in many heart wounds, but they are always present and especially deep and painful when a moral injury has occurred.

DISCUSSION

F | *(5 min) Small group.*

1. How do guilt and shame affect a person's life? Their relationship with God?
2. What are other effects of moral injury?

F | *(14 min) Large group. Get feedback. Add content below that was not mentioned.*

People who suffer from a moral injury may be angry at those who put them in the situation. They may be angry at themselves for having done an evil thing. Even people who do not believe in God may be angry at God for allowing such a terrible experience to happen.

They may feel unforgivable. Even if their actions would not lead to conviction in a court of law, they cannot forgive themselves. And they cannot imagine that God, their loved ones, or society will ever forgive them either. This can lead to isolation and loss of relationships.

Shame makes them want to hide, either physically or emotionally, never letting anyone know about the pain in their soul. They think that anyone who discovers what they did will abandon them, so they keep it secret.

Suffering from a moral injury can lead people to lose hope. They may:

- not be able to trust others.
- not be able to believe the Bible.
- not trust themselves to do what is good.
- try to avoid feeling any emotions so they will not have to feel the painful ones.
- despair to the point of trying to harm themselves or taking their own life.
- not be able to accept help that is offered to them.

Section 4.   20 min

Moral injury and the Bible

F | *(1 min) Present the content below.*

The Bible does not use the term "moral injury" but it does describe many situations in which men and women suffered guilt and shame after they violated their deep sense of what was right, or they witnessed such a violation.

DISCUSSION

F | *(5 min) Small group. Divide the examples among the groups.*

1. In the following examples, how might each of the main characters have felt?
   David: 1 Samuel 22:1–22
   Peter: Matthew 26:34–35, 69–75
   Paul: Acts 8:1–3, 22:4–5; 1 Timothy 1:13–16

2. How did God use them for his purposes afterward?
   David: 2 Samuel 23:1–4
   Peter: John 21:15–19
   Paul: Acts 9:13–16

F | *(14 min) Large group. Get feedback. Add content below that was not mentioned.*

Each of these people may have felt grief, regret, hopelessness, guilt, and shame. They may have felt that God could never use them again for his good purposes. But God is always pursuing us. He loves us and desires a relationship with us and is ready to forgive when we turn back to him. In Matthew 26:69–75, Peter denied knowing Christ and then wept bitterly over his action. But later Jesus restored him (John 21:15–19), and God was able to use him in greater ways for his purposes. Both David and Paul were the cause of harm to others. It grieved them deeply, but God did not give up on them. God always responds with grace to humble, repentant people (Isaiah 57:15; Psalm 51:17; James 4:6).

Section 5.

How can we help someone with moral injury?

DISCUSSION

F | *(5 min) Small group.*

1. If you have known someone with this type of injury, was anything helpful for them? If yes, what?
2. What was not helpful?

F | *(10 min) Large group. Get feedback. Add content below that was not mentioned.*

Here are some things that may help people with moral injury heal.

- Telling their story to someone they trust. The listener should not try to minimize the person's feelings or rush to talk about forgiveness.
- Understanding what moral injury is and how it has impacted them.
- Confessing their actions to someone they respect as a moral or spiritual leader.
- Over time, forgiving themselves and others and beginning to accept the forgiveness God promises (1 John 1:9).
- Reestablishing relationships with family and community and making amends, where possible.
- Spending time helping others and doing useful things for individuals or the community.
- Participating in a community or church ceremony of forgiveness and reintegration.

A moral injury may make it difficult for someone to reach out to others or receive help. What does the Bible teach us about receiving help from others?

DISCUSSION

F | *(5 min) Large group.*

Read these two stories of soldiers who needed help. One needed help for someone he cared about and the other for himself: Matthew 8:5–13; 2 Kings 5:1–14

1. What prompted these people to seek healing?
2. Why might it have been difficult for them to ask for help?

F | *(10 min) Large group. Get feedback. Add content below that was not mentioned.*

In Matthew 8, the centurion sought help for his paralyzed servant, who could not ask for himself. This required love and compassion, and Jesus calls him a man of great faith. Like this servant, hurting people may need intervention from others who care about them.

In 2 Kings 5, Naaman had to reveal his disease of leprosy to select people who could help him. This was difficult for him to do, but it led to healing. For those with heart wounds or moral injuries, it takes courage to name the event and the pain, but this is key to recovering.

DISCUSSION

F | *(5 min) Small group.*

What practical things can your church community do to help people heal from moral injury?

F | *(10 min) Large group. Get feedback. Add content below that was not mentioned.*

Churches should be like hospitals for spiritually and emotionally wounded people. Churches can help by seeking out wounded people and inviting them into relationships where they are respected, loved, listened to, forgiven, and given opportunities to be involved in serving others. This can help them connect with others, which is an important part of healing both heart and soul wounds.

Closing   5 min

F | *Select the verses you would like to read from the list, according to your context and time.*

Close your eyes, if you like, and listen to these verses from the Bible. These things are true about everyone who is in Christ.

Zephaniah 3:17–18   2 Corinthians 5:17–19

Romans 5:8   Ephesians 2:1–10

F | *Close this exercise with a prayer for people with moral injuries to experience God's love for them.*

8. How can we help children who have experienced bad things?

This lesson focuses on children who have been traumatized. The same principles can also apply to normal parenting.

Before you begin:

- For Section 1: Decide how you will present the story (see page 190, "Stories" in "Preparing the lessons").
- For Section 2: Prepare the outline drawing of a child.
- For Section 3: If needed, prepare slips of paper or index cards with Bible verses or download the Bible verses PDF.
- For Section 4: Prepare answers for Question 1.

In this lesson we will:

- Identify when problem behaviors in children are due to trauma and loss.
- Explore ways to respond to children that help them express their pain in words, in play, and in art.
- Discuss how to respond to children according to the Bible; if necessary, challenge the way the culture responds to children.

Section 1: Story	10 min
Section 2: How do children who have experienced bad things behave?	15 min
Section 3: What does our culture and the Bible say about how to treat children?	20 min
Section 4: How do we help children who have experienced bad things?	30 min
Section 5: Special cases	5–15 min
Closing	10 min
Total time	**1 hour 30 – 40 minutes**

8. How can we help children who have experienced bad things?

F | (1 min) Introduce lesson title and objectives. Direct participants to the corresponding lesson in Healing the Wounds of Trauma.

Section 1.   10 min

The story of Kevin

F | (5 min) Large group. Present the story.

Seven-year-old Kevin had never known his real father. He had left Kevin's mother when Kevin was a baby. Kevin was a good boy who always wanted to help. His mother struggled to support him and his younger sister with minimum-wage retail jobs. She had a series of boyfriends who would often stay overnight and who brought alcohol and drugs with them. Sometimes these men would become angry and violent.

One night, Kevin witnessed a man starting to undress and fondle his little sister. His mom, who was drunk, tried clumsily to interfere, but the man beat her off. Kevin rushed in with both arms flailing to protect his sister and his mom from the large man. The last thing he remembered was pain on the right side of his head. His head hit the wall and he fell, unconscious.

He remembers coming to and seeing the police taking the man away in handcuffs and then taking his mother away. A woman told him that she would take him and his sister to a new home to live. He couldn't understand why they couldn't stay with their mom.

The woman they went to live with had another foster child already. She was not very compassionate or understanding. Kevin started wetting the bed nearly every night, something he had not done for a long time. The woman was angry at him. She shouted, "You're too old to wet your bed!" He felt so ashamed.

Kevin got into trouble at school for fighting with other boys. He would not respond to his teacher at all. Kris, the social worker assigned to his case, tried to get Kevin to talk about his feelings, but he just kept quiet. Finally she gave him a piece of paper and markers and asked him to draw something. He drew a picture of violent fighting, with a small boy stabbing a large man.

Kris asked him, "Tell me about what is happening in this picture." Kevin told her about what he remembered on the night of the fight. Then Kris asked, "How did you feel?" Kevin told how he was so afraid. Kris asked, "What was the most difficult part for you?" Kevin began to cry. He said, "I couldn't help my sister!" As Kevin explained the picture, his feelings came out and finally he cried and cried. With Kris's patience and reassurance, he felt safe to share more details of his story. And little by little he began to feel better.

F | *(5 min) Large group.*

1. How did Kevin behave before, during, and after that evening?
2. Why do you think his behavior changed?

F | *If the participants are using books, encourage them to keep them closed as much as possible for the rest of the lesson.*

Section 2.

15 min

8

How do children who have experienced bad things behave?

DISCUSSION

F | *(5 min) Small group. Say, "Think about the child in the story and children you know. How were they affected by the bad things they experienced? I am going to divide you into three groups, each to discuss one of the following questions. Have one person in each group list your responses."*

1. How is a child's behavior affected?
2. How is a child's body affected?
3. How are a child's emotions affected?

Fig. 8.1a: Child outline

F | *(10 min) Large group. Get feedback. Use a large paper with the outline of a child, like the drawing (Fig.8.1a). As you get feedback from each group, write behaviors outside of the body, write physical reactions in the body, and write emotions inside the heart and head. Do not worry if there is overlap between these categories. Add content from A–C that was not mentioned.*

Also say, "If a child suddenly begins showing these changes in behavior, body, or emotions, a parent should try to find out if something bad has happened to them, rather than just disciplining them."

Option: Do this exercise as a large group exercise, using the same process.

A. Their behavior is affected.

*   They may go back to behaving like they did when they were younger. For example, children who had stopped sucking their thumbs may start doing it again.

- In their play they may act out something similar to the bad thing that happened to them.
- They may cry a lot.
- They may be especially upset if they lose things that matter to them, like clothes or a toy or a book.
- They may become quiet and not respond to what is going on around them.
- They may do poorly at school because they cannot concentrate. Or they may refuse to go to school.
- They may not care if they live or die.
- Small children may cling to their parents.
- They may try to take on responsibility for the family and act like adults.
- They may fight a lot and be irritable or aggressive. Small children may fight with their playmates more than before. Older children may rebel against their parents and teachers more than before.
- Older children may use alcohol or drugs to kill their pain or become sexually active.
- Older children may take risks, like riding fast on a motorcycle, taking up a dangerous sport, or becoming a soldier. This makes them feel brave in the face of danger.
- Older children may hurt themselves, for example by cutting their bodies or committing suicide.

B. Their bodies are affected.

- Children who had stopped wetting the bed may start doing it again.
- They may have more nightmares and bad dreams than usual. (Small children who are not traumatized may have "night terrors," where they scream and look awake when they are actually asleep. It will stop as they grow older.)
- Their speech may be affected. They may begin to stutter, or they may become mute.
- They may lose their appetite because they are anxious, or they may eat too much to try to kill the pain.
- They may complain of headaches, stomachaches, or other pain in their bodies. They may have hives or asthma.

C. Their emotions are affected.

- They may be fearful. They may be afraid of things they were not afraid of before. They may fear something bad will happen again.
- They may be angry.
- They may feel confused.
- They may be sad. Even though a child is very sad, such as after someone dies, it is normal for him to stay sad for a while, and then play for a while.
- They may lose interest in life. The pain in their hearts preoccupies their minds. It saps their energy for life.
- They may feel they are responsible for what happened.
- Older children may feel guilty that they survived when others did not.

Section 3. 20 min

What does our culture and the Bible say about how to treat children?

DISCUSSION

F | *(5 min) Large group.*

1. How do parents in your community usually react when their children behave in ways they do not like?
2. Is it the custom in your community that parents talk with their children and listen to them? If not, why not?

DISCUSSION

F | *(5 min) Small group. Distribute the verses among the groups.*

1. Read the verses below and compare what they say with the ways adults treat children in your community.
   Mark 10:13–16   Deuteronomy 6:4–9
   Colossians 3:21   Matthew 18:5–6

2. Which of these cultural ways of treating children are helpful to continue doing and which ways should be changed?

F | *(10 min) Large group. Get feedback. Add content below that was not mentioned.*

Jesus cared deeply for children and got angry when people disregarded them or caused them to sin (Mark 10:13–16; Matthew 18:5–6). Parents are responsible for the spiritual instruction of their children (Deuteronomy 6:4–9). The Bible warns parents against making their children bitter and discouraged (Colossians 3:21). As Christians, we should treat children like Jesus does, even if it goes against our culture.

Section 4. 30 min

How do we help children who have experienced bad things?

F | *Mention section title and present the paragraph below.*

The most important thing parents can do to help their child is to heal from their own heart wounds. They can do this by identifying the wounds of their own hearts, grieving well, and bringing their pain to Jesus. This gives an example for their children to imitate. If parents have not worked through their own heart wounds, it will be hard for them to help their children.

DISCUSSION

F | *(5 min) Large group.*

1. What helped the child at the beginning of the lesson find healing?

F | *(5 min) Small group. After reading Question 2, assign each group one of the sections (A–E) to read and then to create a skit in which one person acts the role of a helpful parent and another acts the role of a child. It should not be more than a few minutes long. If role plays are not familiar to your participants, act out an example first.*

2. What other things can we do to help a child who has experienced bad things?

A. Be patient and gentle.

Children who have experienced bad things may get overwhelmed by their heart wound and misbehave or disobey. They are still feeling the pain. When they are upset, they are not able to think clearly, learn, or change their behavior. This makes parenting more difficult. Instead of immediately scolding or disciplining the child, it is best first to help them calm down by talking gently to them or possibly holding them. When they are calm, they may be able to talk about what is happening and what is causing them to feel angry, afraid, or sad. Even if they cannot talk about it, a calm and understanding response will comfort them.

B. Listen to children's pain.

Children know more about what is going on around them than adults realize. If they do not have a chance to talk about things, they may get strange ideas in their heads. They tend to fill in missing information in whatever way makes sense to them. Even if parents are not used to talking with their children, it is important that they do so when bad things are going on, as well as afterwards. If the child is old enough to give a thoughtful response, use the three listening questions—"What happened? How did you feel? What was the hardest part for you?" This is not the time to say, "Go away and play."

Families should talk together about the bad things that happened. Each child should have the chance to say what they felt when the bad things happened. Even children who are not showing that they have problems may still be suffering. They should have the chance to share their pain. It is also good for parents to talk with each child individually.

Children younger than school age are often better able to express things through playing with objects rather than by answering questions. When children act out a bad event while they are playing, it helps them work out the pain they experienced. Parents should watch the child playing and tell the child what they see, without judgment. This shows they want to understand their child. Older children may be able to answer questions about what they did in their play. Then parents can go from talking about the play to talking about the painful experience.

Another way to help children talk about their pain is through drawing. Parents can give them paper and pencils or chalk, or if these are not available, have them draw in the dirt. Ask them to draw a person, then their family, then where they used to live. Ask them to explain their drawing to you. Remember that the goal is to help them talk about their pain, not to teach or correct them.

If children have bad dreams, explain that many times people dream about bad things that have happened to them. Encourage them to talk about their dreams. Ask them if they think their dream could be related to something that happened to them.

Fig. 8.2: A child's drawing of a painful experience

C. Establish routines.

When the activities of each day are predictable, children recover more quickly. Each day children should know what is likely to happen. They should be encouraged to go to school, do regular chores, and play with their friends. As a family, have a time each day to meet and talk about the day, to read the Bible, pray, and sing together, for example at bedtime. For displaced people, think of routines that can be done where the family is sheltered. Part of the activities should be having fun together. This may be playing games or, if making noise is dangerous, telling stories.

Try to finish activities that have been started. This gives children the sense that they are able to accomplish something. It restores their sense of security, that the future is not out of control.

If families have been separated, try to bring them together quickly after the bad event, if that is possible. However, if children are suffering from domestic abuse, the approach is different: family members need to be protected in a safe location where the abuser will not hurt them.

D. Tell children the truth about the situation.

Children need to understand the truth of what has happened, in ways appropriate for their age. They should be told whether or not there is still danger and whether or not someone has died. Knowing the real danger is better than imagining all sorts of dangers. At the same time, parents should not exaggerate the danger or speak of all the bad things that could possibly happen. Ask the children what questions they have rather than giving information that they may not want or need. Do not show them disturbing photos or describe blood and violence in detail.

Parents should make a plan for what they will do if something else bad happens and discuss it openly with the family.

E. Spend time together with God.

Trauma can disrupt a child's relationship with God. Children may ask questions like, "Why did God let this happen? Was it my fault?" Though some of their questions may be difficult to answer, parents should answer as best and as truthfully as they can. Reading Bible verses that illustrate laments and God's response can bring comfort to children. Children should be allowed to give their prayer requests and to talk to God in their own way. As soon as children can talk to other people, they can talk to God. Praying and singing together can also help children feel loved by God and their parents, and this can help them feel less afraid. The Lord's Prayer or the prayer in Psalm 31:1–3 are good prayers for parents to use with their children.

Memorizing Scripture verses can also help remind children that God is near, and that he cares for them. Some examples are:

- Psalm 121:4: God is a watchman who never sleeps
- 1 Peter 5:7: God can take all our fears
- Psalm 23:1: God takes care of all our needs
- Psalm 46:1: God is always there as our refuge
- Proverbs 3:5: God wants us to trust him
- Matthew 11:29: God is gentle and patient

F | *(10 min) Have each group perform their skit.*

Section 5. Other considerations

F | *(5–15 min) Large group. Depending on your context, choose one or more of the topics in Section 5 and discuss them, using the suggested questions.*

A. Teenagers

F | *Ask, "What are some of the particular needs that teenagers may have after they have experienced bad things?" Add content below that was not mentioned.*

Teenagers go through a difficult period of life even when there are no wars or other trauma. Some problems that may arise after a traumatic situation may be due simply to the age of the child.

Teenagers, especially girls, may have a need for privacy. When families are displaced or in crisis, understanding a teenage girl's need for privacy can help, even if parents are not able to provide her with much privacy.

Teenagers often need to discuss things with their peers. This should be encouraged, especially after a traumatic event. Teenagers also need trusted adults who are not their parents to talk with.

Teenagers need to feel useful, especially when their family is going through difficulties. If they can do things that help their family survive, this will give them a sense of worth.

B. Teachers and school administrators

F | *Ask, "Why would it be important to inform teachers and school administrators about what a child has experienced?" Add content below that was not mentioned.*

Parents and other leaders should arrange a time to meet with the school director and teachers to discuss what has happened. If the teachers understand the situation and how it might affect the child's performance at school, they will be more patient with the student and will be a part of the healing process.

C. Serious cases

F | *Ask, "How would you know if a child needs special help?" Add content below that was not mentioned.*

If a child is still showing serious problems after some time or is harming other people or themselves, some wise person needs to spend a lot of time with that child. He or she may need professional help from someone trained as a counselor. God can heal the child, but it will take time and extra care.

Special help is also needed for former child soldiers and gang members. They will suffer trauma and may not develop properly as an adult without a lot of help. They have seen many evil acts and may have learned to use violence as a way of solving life's problems. They may have been forced to do terrible things against their own communities or families. If possible, they need to return to their families, but this may be difficult because of what they have done. People may be afraid of them or hate them.

Before they are able to return to normal life, they will need to know that people love and care for them. The church needs to help the community recognize the pain, loss, and trauma these children have experienced. Both the community and these children need to give their pain to God, so he can heal them. They need to confess their sins, forgive each other, and be reconciled (1 John 1:8–9). All this may take many years of effort and prayer.

Closing   10 min

F | *(10 min) Pairs. In pairs, have participants discuss the questions and pray for each other and for the children they know who are in need.*

1. Of the ways to help children that we have discussed, which do you think you could start doing to help them right away?
2. What challenges do you think you will face?
3. What's one thing you want to remember from this lesson?

9. Rape and other forms of sexual assault

Before you begin:

- Tell participants ahead of time that you will be covering this lesson. Let them know that if they are uncomfortable attending, they do not have to attend.
- If you have both men and women in your session, try to have a male and female facilitator leading the session. If this is not possible, study the lesson in advance with a mature Christian of the other gender who will be in the group. Prepare them specifically to lead the discussions in Section 3.
- For Section 1: Choose someone who is familiar with the story to read it. Do not act this story out. Acting out a sexual assault story can be disturbing for some and may trigger painful responses.
- For Section 3: Decide if you will choose Option 1 or Option 2 for the discussions and prepare accordingly.
- For Section 4: Find out what medical and legal help is available for sexual assault victims in the area.
- For Section 4: Read the statement on Confidentiality (page 191). Find out the legal requirements for reporting sexual assault in the area. In most countries, caregivers are obliged by law to report any cases of abuse of a minor. If not reported, there may be legal consequences.
- Recognize that you may have both perpetrators and victims in your group. Some may be both. This lesson focuses on the experience of the victim. Use the addendum about perpetrators if appropriate for your group (page 97).

In this lesson we will:

- Define rape and other forms of sexual assault.
- Explain the way rape and other forms of sexual assault affect a person and their family members.
- Discuss ways to help people who have experienced sexual assault heal from their trauma.
- Discuss ways to help communities accept and nurture children born of rape.

Section 1: Story	25 min
Section 2: What are rape and sexual assault?	5 min
Section 3: What are the effects of rape and sexual assault?	35 min
Section 4: How can we help someone heal?	30 min
Section 5: What about children born as a result of rape?	10 min
Closing	5 min
Total time	**1 hour 50 minutes**

9. Rape and other forms of sexual assault

F | (1 min) Introduce lesson title and objectives. Direct participants to the corresponding lesson in Healing the Wounds of Trauma. Present the paragraph below.

This is a sensitive topic. If you begin to feel uncomfortable at any time and a break would be helpful, please feel free to leave the room. Someone can go with you, listen, and even pray with you, if you would like that.

Section 1.   25 min

The story of Amnon and Tamar

F | (5 min) Large group. Present the story.

Amnon was King David's firstborn son and first in line for the throne. He became so obsessed with his half-sister Tamar that he became ill. She was a virgin, and Amnon thought he could never have her.

When his cousin saw how sad he was, he said to Amnon, "What's the trouble? Why should the son of a king look so dejected morning after morning?"

So Amnon told him, "I am in love with Tamar."

"Well," his cousin said, "Go back to bed and pretend you are ill. When your father comes to see you, ask him to let Tamar come and prepare some food for you."

When the king came to see him, Amnon did just as his cousin had told him. So King David sent Tamar to Amnon's house to prepare some food for him.

When Tamar arrived at Amnon's house, she went to the place where he was lying down and prepared his favorite food for him. But when she set the serving tray before him, he refused to eat. "Everyone get out of here," Amnon told his servants. So they all left.

Then he said to Tamar, "Now bring the food into my bedroom and feed it to me here." So Tamar took his favorite dish to him. But as she was feeding him, he grabbed her and demanded, "Come to bed with me, my darling sister."

"No, my brother!" she cried. "Don't be foolish! Don't do this to me! Such wicked things aren't done in Israel. Where could I go in my shame? And you would be called one of the greatest fools in Israel. Please, just ask the king and he will let you marry me."

But Amnon wouldn't listen to her, and since he was stronger than she was, he raped her. Then suddenly Amnon's love turned to hate, and he hated her even more than he had loved her. "Get out of here!" he snarled at her.

"No, no!" Tamar cried. "Sending me away now is worse than what you've already done to me."

But Amnon wouldn't listen to her. He shouted for his servant and demanded, "Throw this woman out, and lock the door behind her!"

So the servant put her out. She was wearing a long, beautiful robe. But now Tamar tore her robe and put ashes on her head. Then, with her face in her hands, she went away crying.

Her brother Absalom saw her and asked, "Is it true that Amnon has been with you? Well, my sister, keep quiet for now, since he's your brother. Don't you worry about it." So Tamar remained a desolate woman in her brother Absalom's house.

When King David heard what had happened, he was very angry, but he did not do anything to punish Amnon because Amnon was his favorite son.

Absalom hated Amnon deeply because of what he had done and decided he would kill him. Two years later, he was able to trick Amnon and kill him. Afterward, he had to run for his life to another country to escape his father's anger. He stayed there for three years. Finally, David called for him to come back to Jerusalem. But even then, David refused to see him. Absalom became bitter against David and tried to take the throne from him. He died in the attempt. This made King David even sadder. *(Summary of 2 Samuel 13 ff.)*

DISCUSSION

F | *(5 min) Small groups or pairs. Divide questions among the groups. Have each group select someone to take notes and speak for the group. (If possible, have the group select a different person for each small group discussion going forward.)*

1. What effects did this rape have on Tamar? On Amnon? On the family?
2. What in this story shows that Tamar's family was not a safe place for her?
3. What do you think about how David handled this situation?
4. In your culture, how is a victim of rape treated?

F | *(15 min) Large group. Get feedback. If the participants are using books, encourage them to keep them closed as much as possible for the rest of the lesson.*

Section 2. What is rape? What is sexual assault?   5 min

F | *(5 min) Large group. Ask the group to define sexual assault. Then define rape, as a type of sexual assault. If needed, read the definitions provided. Add the other content in this section that was not mentioned.*

Sexual assault is when a person forces themselves sexually on another person. Types of sexual assault include unwanted touching of the private parts of the body, attempted rape, rape, and forcing a victim to perform sexual acts. Specifically, rape is penetrating a person's anus, vagina, or mouth without their consent.

Rape and other forms of sexual assault use physical force, manipulation, or threats to do harm if the victim does not cooperate. It can happen to a woman, girl, man, or boy. The perpetrator may be male or female.

Sexual assault is usually committed by someone who is known and trusted but may also be committed by a stranger. Even during times of peace, sexual assault is a problem, but in times of war it is far more frequent.

While sexual assault may contain an element of sexual desire, it is primarily about power and control. Sometimes its main purpose is to humiliate an individual or a community.

Section 3.

What are the effects of rape and other forms of sexual assault?

F | *(1 min) Mention section title. Present the paragraph below.*

Sexual assault affects every part of a person's life and leaves deep wounds that last a long time. Because victims feel ashamed by the assault, they often keep it secret. Just because a person does not talk about it does not mean it has not happened.

F | *The discussion questions in Section 3 need to be treated differently if you have both men and women in your group. Choose one of the following options depending on your context.*

> 1. *Separate into a men's group and a women's group for the two questions in Section 3 and the two questions in Section 3C. If possible, a male facilitator should lead the men's group and a female facilitator should lead the women's group. If this is not possible, be sure there is a mature Christian in each group who understands the lesson in advance. This helps avoid having participants share things with the large group later that would be hurtful to the other gender and would make them feel unsafe. Bring the whole group back together to read their statements from Question 2 in Section 3C to each other.*
> 2. *Stay in mixed-gender groups for Questions 1 and 2 in Section 3 and Question 1 in Section 3C. Separate into a men's group and a women's group for Question 2 in Section 3C. Bring the whole group together to read their statements from this question to each other.*

DISCUSSION

F | *(5 min) Tell participants that this discussion will first focus on the effects of rape, then later on the effects of other forms of sexual assault. Depending on the size of your group, consider giving Question 1 to some groups and giving Question 2 to other groups.*

1. If a person is raped, how does it affect him or her?
2. What are the effects on the victim's marriage or family?

F | *(15 min) Get feedback on Question 1. Add content from A that was not mentioned. Also ask, "How are the effects of rape different for a man or a woman? A child?" if these topics were not mentioned. Then get feedback on Question 2. Add content from B that was not mentioned.*

A. The effects of rape on victims

Physical
- They may have sexually transmitted infections, injured sexual organs, or other physical injuries.
- They may be on alert all the time.

Emotional
- They may feel a deep sense of shame, dirtiness, and that there's something wrong with them.
- They may feel ruined, that they no longer have any value and are no longer desirable.
- They may try to minimize the pain, deny it, or try to forget about it.
- They may feel guilty, that they deserved it, or that they brought it upon themselves.
- They may be very sad. They may numb their feelings with alcohol, drugs, or food.
- They may try to take their life.
- They may become angry at people. For example, raped women may be angry at all men.
- They may become abusers themselves and try to hurt others in the same way they have been hurt.
- They may be afraid to tell anyone, especially if telling may lead to being killed or bringing shame on the family.
- They may feel helpless and confused.
- They may be afraid of sex or no longer be able to enjoy it. They may begin having sex with many people. It may affect their sexuality in other ways.

Spiritual
- They may think God is punishing them.
- They may be angry at God and unable to trust God to protect them.
- They may think demons have possessed them.

Effects specific to female victims, which can vary by culture:
- They may not be able to get married.
- They may be forced to marry their rapist.
- If they become pregnant from the rape, they may consider abortion.
- They may be killed in an effort to remove shame from the family.
- They may believe this is "just part of being a woman."

Effects specific to male victims:
- They may become confused about their identity as men.
- They may be even more ashamed than female victims.

If an adult was raped as a child, and he or she never received help, the recovery is more difficult.

B. The effects of rape on the victim's marriage and family

If the rape was done by a stranger, the family and community may feel compassionate toward the victim. If they witnessed the rape, they may feel as violated as the victim.

If the victim keeps their rape a secret:
- his or her loved ones will not be able to understand why they are sad and angry.
- his or her spouse may not understand why having sex is so difficult now.

If the victim talks about the rape and it was done by someone the family members know, this can lead to other problems:

- The family may not accept that this person has done such a bad thing.
- If they believe that it happened, they may blame and punish the victim. In some cultures, they may even kill the victim.
- They may be afraid to confront the rapist, especially if the person is a respected member of the community.
- To keep the peace, they may deny that it happened and accuse the victim of lying.
- They may plan how to take revenge.

If a married woman is raped, her husband:

- may fear getting a sexually transmitted disease.
- may feel his wife is now polluted and no longer want to be with her, adding to her feelings of shame and isolation.

9

C. The effects of other types of sexual assault on victims

F | *(4 min) Large group. Add content below that was not mentioned.*

1. How are the effects of other types of sexual assault the same as the effects of rape? How are they different?

The effects of other types of sexual assault may be the same as the effects of rape, to varying degrees. These effects are more easily dismissed by the victim and others. The victim may feel alone and confused, which increases their pain. There also may be less legal help for the victim.

F | *(5 min) Small group. If doing Option 2, separate now into a men's group and a women's group for the following discussion.*

2. What would you like to say to the other group about rape and sexual assault? Write down your response and choose the most appropriate person to read it to the large group.

F | *(5 min) Bring everyone back together. Have a spokesperson from each group read their response from Question 2 to the whole group. Be alert during the feedback to any comments that might hurt someone and intervene as needed.*

Section 4.   30 min

How can we help someone heal from rape or other forms of sexual assault?

F | *(1 min) Mention section title. Present the content below.*

To help victims heal from rape or other forms of sexual assault, allow them to make as many decisions for themselves as possible. This helps restore the power and voice that the perpetrator took or tried to take from them.

DISCUSSION

F | *(5 min) Small group. Divide the questions among the groups.*

1. What kind of medical and legal help do sexual assault victims need? Which of these resources are available in your area?
2. What kind of emotional and spiritual help do they need?

F | *(24 min) Large group. Get feedback. Add content from A and B that was not mentioned. Present section C.*

A. Encourage them to get medical care and legal help.

Medical care:

- Contact a sexual assault or rape crisis center in your area, if there is one. If the victim is considered an adult by the laws of the country, be sure to ask his or her permission. A crisis center will know the best steps to take to care of the victim.
- Get medical care as soon as possible. Even if there is a delay, medical care is still worthwhile.
- A doctor should check for infections and injuries like broken bones or internal bleeding.
- Medicines can be given immediately or soon after a rape that make it less likely that the person will contract HIV or other sexually transmitted diseases. These medicines are different from those that reject a possible pregnancy.
- If a victim finds out she is pregnant, she will need special help.

Legal help:

- Rape is a crime in most countries, as are many other types of sexual assault.
- Report to the police. If the victim is an adult, they need to agree to report. They are not always ready to do this. Someone who has experience in this area can talk with them and help them decide what to do.
- Most countries require anyone who knows about the rape of a minor to report it to the police.

Someone the victim trusts should go with him or her to the doctor and the police. This provides comfort and support. Often they are asked uncomfortable questions by the police or doctor.

B. Provide emotional and spiritual help

Emotional help:

- Victims need to talk with someone they trust, someone who will keep the matter private. Allow them to choose who they want to meet with.
- They need listeners who can create a safe space for them to express anything, including anger, sadness, sexual concerns, and doubts about their faith. These people need to listen without correcting or blaming the victim.

- Victims need listeners who are patient and committed, since heart wounds caused by sexual assault can take a long time to heal. Listeners should help victims realize the impact the sexual assault has had on their lives.
- They need listeners who are aware that a close bond can form between them and the victim. A listener needs to ensure this bond does not become inappropriate. If the listener is of the opposite sex, another trusted person should be present.

Spiritual help:

- Victims may blame God for not protecting them or feel so angry with God that they are not willing to pray, listen to God's Word, or hear talk about God's love for them, at least at first. This is normal.
- Victims need people who are simply willing to show God's love to them. When they see that these people still value and love them, they will gradually realize that they are not ruined. Spouses and family members can play a key role in this.
- Victims need to know it is okay for them to feel angry with God. He understands and still loves and accepts them. It is better for them to be truthful about their feelings than to hide them. Writing a lament can be a way to get the feelings out (see "Laments" in the Grief lesson).
- Eventually, they may be willing to receive comfort from God's Word and have others pray for them. Some Scriptures that may be helpful are Psalm 9:9–10 and Psalm 10:17–18.
- When victims are ready, they can bring their pain to God in prayer and ask God for healing. They should be encouraged to be specific in telling God what they lost in the sexual assault—for example, innocence, purity, joy. They can ask God to restore these things to them (Psalm 71:20–21).

Victims can be helped by a supportive church community. Church leaders can:

- Address sexual assault in sermons and pray for victims. This can bring hope to those who have kept their assault secret and may help them be willing to talk with someone about it.
- Identify people in the church who are good listeners and give them training to improve their skills.
- Lead their congregations in the practice of lament, so that people know it is okay to express their anger and pain to God.

C. Support them in the difficult process of forgiveness

When God begins to heal the pain in victims' hearts, they can begin the difficult work of forgiving their perpetrator. This is not easy, and it may take a long time. It does not mean that the perpetrator does not have to face the consequences of their act. People can genuinely forgive and still bring the perpetrator to court. Forgiveness may not result in reconciliation. It may never be safe to be in relationship with the perpetrator again.

If the perpetrator goes unpunished, it makes forgiving him or her even more difficult. It can be a comfort for victims to remember that God hates injustice and will avenge the wrong that has been done to them (Isaiah 61:8a; Isaiah 59:14–19).

Section 5.

What about children born as a result of rape?

F | *Mention section title.*

DISCUSSION

F | *(3 min) Small group.*

Are there any children in your church or community who are teased or rejected because of the events surrounding their birth? If so, how are you helping them?

F | *(7 min) Large group. Get feedback. Then cover points A and B briefly.*

A. What are their needs?

Sometimes, children born as a result of rape are rejected by their families, especially their mothers. They may be treated poorly, or even neglected so much that they die. They may be ridiculed for not having a father. Their siblings may not consider them to be full members of the family.

B. How can we help these children?

God has a special love for the fatherless (Deuteronomy 10:18). In Psalm 68:5–6a, it says: "God, who lives in his sacred Temple, cares for orphans and protects widows. He gives the lonely a home to live in and leads prisoners out into happy freedom." As Christians, we should ask God to help us love these children in the same way God loves them. They need our love even more than other children. They need special teaching from God's Word to assure them that their life is not an accident. Some Scriptures that might be helpful are Psalm 139:13–18 and Isaiah 49:15. These children are not responsible for the conditions of their birth.

When they begin to ask who their father is, tell them the truth, in a way that is appropriate for their age. If available, someone who has a lot of experience working with children can help us know how to talk about this.

Welcoming a child of rape is an example of how God welcomes us regardless of our background. Church leaders can help the family and church community accept the child. They can ask a special blessing on the baby and the family at the dedication or baptism. This needs to be done carefully so it does not bring more shame on the family.

Closing

F | *(5 min) Give participants time to write their answer for Question 1, then have them discuss Question 2 in pairs and pray. After the pairs have prayed, pray for the group as a whole, including the verse Psalm 56:8 in your prayer.*

1. What's one thing you want to remember from this lesson?
2. Share this with each other in pairs, then pray for each other.

You keep track of all my sorrows.
You have collected all my tears in your bottle.
You have recorded each one in your book. (Psalm 56:8 NLT)

Addendum: **20 min**

What do perpetrators need?

Perpetrators need to repent of their sin and connect to the community. The church can help with this.

A. Perpetrators need to genuinely repent and demonstrate it by their behavior

DISCUSSION

> F | *(7 min) Large group. After the discussion, add content below the question that was not mentioned.*

What are signs that a person has begun the process of true repentance?

Honest admission:
- They tell themselves and others the truth about what they have done.
- They feel remorse for what they have done.
- They take responsibility for the hurt they have caused.
- They search for the roots of their desire to have power over others.
- They confess their sin to God and accept God's forgiveness.

Sustained efforts to repair the harm done:
- If the victim is willing to speak with them, they ask the victim for forgiveness.
- They show their repentance in deed as appropriate (Numbers 5:5–7; Luke 3:8; Luke 19:8; Acts 26:20b).
- They accept that it takes time to rebuild trust.
- They accept that reconciliation may never be possible.

Willing acceptance of discipline and supervision:
- They make themselves fully accountable to another person.
- They accept the legal and social consequences for what they have done.
- If they are part of a church, they inform the pastor about what they have done and submit to any restrictions the church puts in place to protect the innocent.

B. Perpetrators need to experience community in a way that is safe for them and others

DISCUSSION

> F | *(6 min) Large group. After the discussion, add content below that was not mentioned.*

How could a church provide perpetrators of sexual assault opportunities for community in a way that is safe for them and others?

Perpetrators of sexual assault need meaningful connection to community. If they are left isolated and alone, it is more likely that they will harm others again. A church can assign a team of mature members who can meet regularly with the person and disciple them.

Even if people have genuinely repented of sexual assault, churches should take measures to make sure that vulnerable people are never alone with them. This is also true for perpetrators who were leaders in the church. In the same way that Israel's priests were to be removed from leadership when they committed sin and led the people astray, so these church leaders should be removed from leadership. If they demonstrate genuine repentance, they may be able to be assigned other tasks to serve God's people, as Israel's priests were (Ezekiel 44:10–14).

C. Perpetrators need to heal from their heart wounds if they have been victims themselves.

F | *(1 min) Large group. Present the content below.*

Some perpetrators have been victims of sexual assault or abuse. They may need help such as found in Section 4 above.

10. HIV and AIDS

Before you begin:

- For Section 1: Decide if you will use the skit or the story, depending upon which is most appropriate in your context. If you choose the skit, prepare the signs and find 10 participants who are willing to play the roles. If you choose the story, decide how you will present it (see page 190, "Stories" in "Preparing the lessons").
- If possible, find an informed medical person who can be present during this session, particularly during Section 3.
- Decide if you will include Section 4. (See timesaver note under that section.)

In this lesson we will:

- Explain how a person is infected with HIV and how that can develop into AIDS.
- Identify beliefs and practices that contribute to the spread of HIV and find ways to address them.
- Discuss ways to prevent HIV.
- Learn how to help the church come alongside those affected by HIV and AIDS.

Section 1: Skit or story	15 min
Section 2: What do you know about HIV and AIDS?	15 min
Section 3: What are some false beliefs that increase the spread of HIV?	15 min
Section 4: What are some practices that increase the spread of HIV?	10 min
Section 5: How can we keep HIV from spreading?	15 min
Section 6: How can we help people who are HIV positive?	15 min
Closing	20 min
Total time	**1 hour 45 minutes**

10. HIV and AIDS

F | *This lesson is not a medical recommendation for diagnosis or treatment of HIV. Diagnosis and treatment should be done by a health care provider knowledgeable about the disease. Be aware that treatment recommendations may change over time. This lesson uses antiretroviral (ARV) medications as an example of a current treatment of HIV. ARVs help to control HIV infection and can prolong life but do not cure it.*

(1 min) Introduce lesson title and objectives. Direct participants to the corresponding lesson in Healing the Wounds of Trauma.

Section 1. A skit or a story   15 min

Blood wars skit

F | *Beforehand, prepare signs people can pin to themselves or hang around their necks. The signs say: "HIV" (x2), "flu," "malaria," "pneumonia," "diarrhea," "blood soldier" (x2), and "ARV" (x2). Substitute another disease for malaria if that is not a problem in your area.*

(5 min) Act out the skit:

1. Designate a large space on the floor as the body of Mark.
2. Designate participants to act out the following parts and give each one the appropriate sign to wear. (Note: In some contexts physical contact of men and women in public is not allowed. In these contexts, have either all men or all women playing the skit parts.)
   - Two blood soldiers. They can pretend they are armed.
   - Two HIV virus.
   - One for each illness: flu, malaria, pneumonia, diarrhea.
   - Two ARV soldiers
3. Say the following, as participants act out a and b: God has created us with blood soldiers to protect us. Mark has his blood soldiers in his body that will fight against sicknesses. Their job is to protect Mark from illnesses. They must prowl around looking for intruders.
   a. The blood soldiers prowl around Mark's body looking for any sickness that tries to enter.
   b. Invite **Flu** to invade—he is quickly thrown out *(do not be too violent)*. Ask **Malaria** to invade—he is thrown out after a short struggle.
4. Say: Everyone freeze. Then say the following, as participants act out a and b: Mark is doing fine and is able to defeat diseases using his blood soldiers. Now Mark went and slept with someone other than his wife.
   a. Two **HIVs** sneak in without the blood soldiers noticing and hide.
   b. **Flu** returns—and is thrown out as quickly as happened earlier. Now have **Malaria** invade—he too is thrown out after a little struggle.

5. Say: Everyone freeze. Then say the following, as participants act out a, b, and c: Mark does not realize he is ill. He is, however, infectious and can spread HIV to other people. Now time passes and it is a year later.
   a. Now one **HIV** stands up and holds one of the blood soldiers so he cannot do anything.
   b. **Flu** returns and there is a struggle. **Pneumonia** joins in. It takes a long struggle for the remaining blood soldier to throw them out.
   c. The other **HIV** stands up and holds the remaining blood soldier. **Flu, Pneumonia, Malaria,** and **Diarrhea** invade Mark's body. The blood soldiers are held down and **Flu** and all the other illnesses have a dance of victory around the body of Mark.
6. Say: Everyone freeze. Then say the following, as participants act out a: Mark now has AIDS. HIV, a tiny virus, has disabled his body's ability to fight infection, so many other illnesses invade. AIDS is not one disease but a combination of diseases. Finally the person wastes away. Now let us see what happens when ARV drugs are used.
   a. Two **ARVs** now come into Mark's body. They hold down **HIV** so now when **Flu, Malaria,** etc. invade the blood soldiers can throw them out.
7. Say: Everyone freeze. Then say: Blood tests are important—the only way to be sure of recognizing HIV infection. ARVs are drugs that do not rid the body of HIV but control it. The medicine has to be taken life long; if stopped the HIV will escape and will again cause trouble.

DISCUSSION

F | (5 min) Small group. Have each group select someone to take notes and speak for the group. (If possible, have the group select a different person for each small group discussion going forward.)

1. In your area, do people tell others if they know they have HIV or AIDS? Why or why not?
2. How do people in your community treat people with HIV or AIDS?

F | (5 min) Large group. Get feedback. If the participants are using books, encourage them to keep them closed as much as possible for the rest of the lesson.

The story of Gabriel and Sarah

F | (5 min) Large group. Present the story.

Gabriel and Sarah had married very young, just after high school. Although they decided to continue their studies at community college, Sarah became pregnant and decided to dedicate herself full time to taking care of her little Hannah. Gabriel worked hard as a sales rep for an IT company and always got "top employee" awards. Recently the company had been bought by a national company, and Gabriel was promoted to a regional position that paid twice the salary.

"Three weeks on the road and only one with you and Hannah…how will we manage?" Gabriel asked Sarah.

"I know. But it's such an opportunity for you, for us, right?" she replied. "We could even save enough to buy a home."

After a year, they were financially comfortable. They had replaced their second-hand furniture with nicer things. And most exciting, they were expecting their second child.

However, the time on the road was hard for Gabriel. He was really lonely, especially in the evenings. He didn't go to the bars with his younger coworkers who often traveled with him. But then Diana was assigned to the team. She was easy to talk to, and they became friends. Little by little they got caught up in a torrid romance that lasted a month, until she was transferred to another region. Gabriel was wracked with guilt and decided he would never do anything like this again… and would never tell Sarah, because it would break her heart.

After a couple of years, Gabriel began to experience health problems—fatigue, weight loss, and diarrhea. Sarah, who was pregnant for the third time, was really concerned and insisted that he take a medical leave and schedule all the tests the doctor had ordered.

"I regret to inform you that you are HIV positive," said the doctor. Shock and numbness engulfed him, and then grief, as he remembered Diana. He realized he had to tell Sarah the whole truth; there was no other way. And her HIV test turned out positive, too. For weeks, Sarah alternated between rage, unbelief, and sobbing, as she tried to absorb the diagnosis and the story about Diana. Both she and Gabriel started taking special medicine called ARVs, to control the HIV infection. The doctor said the medicine would enable them to live fairly healthy lives, but there was no cure for HIV. Sarah also took special medicines so that the baby would be less likely to be born HIV-positive.

Sarah had become very involved in her church over the years. She was so ashamed to tell Rebecca, the small group leader, about the diagnosis and the story behind it, but she knew she couldn't walk this road alone. Rebecca listened compassionately as Sarah wept out the story, and assured her, "We will not leave you alone in this journey, Sarah. We will be with you and your family at every step." Rebecca helped her contact a local agency that provided support and advice to people with HIV, and the agency answered all of Sarah and Gabriel's questions and provided counseling as they processed their grief. Sarah and Gabriel also began seeing a counselor so they could start working through the devastating impact of Gabriel's affair.

When their baby girl was born healthy, Sarah wept with relief. They named her "Hope." Amidst all the pain and grief, Hope was a ray of light.

DISCUSSION

F | (5 min) Small group. Have each group select someone to take notes and speak for the group. (If possible, have the group select a different person for each small group discussion going forward.)

1. In your area, do people tell others if they know they have HIV or AIDS? Why or why not?
2. How do people in your community treat people with HIV or AIDS?

F | (5 min) Large group. Get feedback. If the participants are using books, encourage them to keep them closed as much as possible for the rest of the lesson.

Section 2. What do you know about HIV and AIDS?   **15 min**

F | *(15 min) Mention section title. Read the questions aloud and have each person write down their answers. Then go over the correct answers (last page of lesson). Discuss anything that is not clear. See how many people got all the answers correct, how many missed just one, and so forth. See "Mother-to-child transmission of HIV" (footnote).*

QUIZ

1. What does AIDS stand for?
2. What does HIV stand for?
3. What are the three fluids that can carry HIV?
4. What is the most frequent way that people worldwide are infected with HIV?
5. Is there a cure for HIV or AIDS?
6. Is it possible for you to be infected with HIV by doing the following? Mark each one yes or no.
   a. Shaking hands with someone infected with HIV.
   b. Receiving an injection with an unsterilized needle.
   c. Sharing food from the same bowl with someone with HIV.
   d. Using the same toilet as someone who has HIV.
   e. Using a razor blade that has been used by another person who has HIV.
   f. Having sex with someone who has HIV.
   g. Hugging a person with AIDS.
   h. Washing the sores of someone who has HIV without wearing gloves.
7. Can you tell by looking that someone has HIV or AIDS?
8. What is the only way to tell for sure if you have HIV?

Answers to quiz on last page of lesson.

Mother-to-child transmission of HIV

1. Normally, the HIV virus does not pass through the placenta. But if the placenta is torn or bleeding, the mother's blood containing HIV can get to the baby.
2. If a mother is HIV positive and not treated, the baby can get HIV by swallowing infected vaginal fluid during the birth process. The virus can also enter through the eyes or through cuts or sores in the skin.
3. Breast milk can be a problem if the baby is eating other food as well, because the food can cause tiny cuts in the stomach lining and HIV can pass through these cuts. If the baby is only receiving breast milk, there is no danger of infection as the milk passes through the baby without damage to the stomach lining. The benefits of breast milk are greater than the risk of transmission. So the advice often given is for the mother to breastfeed for six months with no food given, then stop completely and give the baby food.

Section 3.

What are some false beliefs that increase the spread of HIV?

F | *Mention section title.*

DISCUSSION

F | *(10 min) Small group.*

What do people in your culture believe about the spread of HIV?

F | *(5 min) Large group. Get feedback. Add content below that was not mentioned. Invite someone who is medically trained, such as a doctor or nurse, to help you know if these are true.*

Some people believe things that are not true about sex, HIV, and AIDS. These lies keep them from protecting themselves from HIV. Here are some of them:

- "A man who does not have sex for some time will go mad or become impotent." Or, "Young people need sex to develop normally." Or, "Having sex will help a man get over an illness." These things are not true. Men do not need to have sex to develop normally, recover from illness, be sane, or remain fertile. Jesus and Paul were both celibate.
- "A woman should prove she is fertile before marriage." A woman's value is not based on her ability to bear children. Children are a blessing, but they are not necessary for a Christian marriage. God's plan for marriage when he created it is that the couple be faithful to each other and never have sexual relations with anyone else (Hebrews 13:4).
- "If Satan tempts you to sexual sin, you can't resist." The Bible says, "Resist the Devil and he will run away from you" (James 4:7). God will always give you a way to escape temptation. 1 Corinthians 10:13 says: "Every test that you have experienced is the kind that normally comes to people. But God keeps his promise, and he will not allow you to be tested beyond your power to remain firm; at the time you are put to the test, he will give you the strength to endure it, and so provide you with a way out."
- "AIDS is a curse from God" or "AIDS is caused by witchcraft." There is no mystery about how a person contracts it. It is spread through contact with blood or certain body fluids.
- "If a man has sex with a virgin girl, he will be cured of HIV/AIDS." There is no cure at present for HIV/AIDS and this is a cruel, false idea.

Section 4.

What are some practices that increase the spread of HIV?

F | *Mention section title. **Timesaver**: Section 4 can be skipped, as it is partially covered in Section 3. Or, have some table groups discuss beliefs and other table groups discuss practices.*

DISCUSSION

F | *(5 min) Small group.*

Are there practices in your culture that increase the spread of HIV? What are they?

F | *(5 min) Large group. Get feedback. Add content below that was not mentioned.*

Behaviors or customs that favor the spread of HIV are:
- Having sex with multiple partners.
- Having unprotected sex.
- A low status of women that denies them the freedom to make choices about health care and having sex.
- Sharing injection needles with others.
- Using the same blade to shave people's heads or beards.
- Funeral practices that involve contact with body fluids of the dead person.
- Circumcision using the same blade on one person after another.
- Wife inheritance (for example, a man may be obliged to marry the widow of his dead brother). If the dead brother died of AIDS, the widow will possibly bring HIV into her new family.

Section 5.

How can we keep HIV from spreading?

F | *(5 min) Small groups.*

DISCUSSION

How can we keep HIV from spreading?

F | *(10 min) Large group. Get feedback. Add content below that was not mentioned. (If time permits, ask how and when sex is taught to children and when it would be appropriate to teach about HIV/AIDS.)*

- Teach the idea of "one man for one woman." Having many sexual partners increases the chances of getting HIV and is displeasing to God.
- Teach abstinence before marriage. Some agencies promote the use of condoms as a way to avoid contracting HIV. Condoms reduce the probability of getting HIV, but abstinence before marriage is the only completely safe way to avoid sexual transmission of HIV. It also follows the biblical teaching of reserving sex for marriage (1 Corinthians 6:13b–20). This teaching may challenge traditional sexual practices so young people will need a lot of encouragement to save sex for marriage. The example of the adults will speak louder than any teaching that is given. Groups of young people who promise together to abstain from sex before marriage are more likely to stick to this than individuals who promise something to themselves.
- Use clean needles and cutting instruments.
- Teach children about how HIV spreads. The most likely way a young person will get infected with HIV is through sexual activity. The church needs to help those who teach children about sex know the facts about HIV and AIDS. They should begin educating children about these things before they become sexually active, or earlier if they ask questions. If possible, get books that teach children about sex, HIV, and AIDS.
- Involve youth in HIV prevention: Youth have a lot of energy. Youth can develop ways to teach HIV awareness to others, through drama, song, presentations, or Bible study. They can visit the sick and read Scripture to them. They can do practical things like bringing water or food. When the church involves youth in caring for people with AIDS, it helps the youth to feel wanted and needed. It also helps the youth understand the dangers of getting HIV.

Section 6.   15 min

How can we help people who are HIV-positive?

F | *(1 min) Present the paragraph below.*

Having an HIV diagnosis no longer means that a person will necessarily die from the disease. If diagnosed, treated properly, and given proper support, a person with HIV can live a full life. As we try to help people with HIV, it is important to focus on how they can live positively rather than focusing on death.

DISCUSSION

F | *(14 min) Large group. Read the question and brainstorm answers with "popcorn" responses (quick responses, one after another). Add content from A–F that was not mentioned.*

How can we help people who are HIV-positive?

A. Help them connect to community

People need other people! Those living with HIV/AIDS may be rejected by their friends and even their family. The church needs to work with the community to help them accept people suffering with this illness and not be afraid of them. By providing community, we can help meet the person's emotional needs. Those who are living with HIV/AIDS can help each other by meeting and sharing their experiences. The church could help to arrange this. The church can also include people living with HIV/AIDS in church activities, because people who have a sense of purpose will live longer than those who do not.

B. Help them tell others about their illness.

Often people want to hide that they are HIV-positive. This does not help the sick person or the community. If they do not tell the real reason they are sick, people may wrongly accuse others of having caused the illness through a curse or witchcraft. It takes a brave person to be the first to say publicly that he or she has HIV or AIDS, but this can help others to do so.

C. Help them understand the grief process.

When someone has a chronic disease, they experience great loss and additional heart wounds. They often go through the stages of grief: anger and denial, loss of hope, and then new beginnings. People who help them need to know that it is normal to be angry at first. They may also deny that they have HIV. They may lose hope, and it may take months before they can accept their situation. They may bargain with God, promising certain behaviors in exchange for their health. They will need extra support as they process their heart wounds (2 Corinthians 1:3–5).

D. Help them care for their bodies.

A person with HIV can live a long time if they take care of their bodies. If they are able to take antiviral drugs, they must follow the doctor's instructions exactly. If used properly, these drugs can extend their life by many years. Good regular food will help people fight off disease. It is particularly important that sick people eat plenty of fruit and vegetables so that they get good vitamins to keep their bodies healthy. They will need a lot of rest, and they should not smoke, or drink much alcohol. When they get sick with other diseases, they must go for treatment immediately.

Fig. 10.1: Caring for someone with HIV

10

E. Ensure that they and their families are provided for

Help the person connect with programs that can help them earn income and provide for their family. The family may need practical support for their daily needs (Matthew 25:35–40).

Helping a person write a will can protect the spouse and children from extended family or others taking the house, land, or other assets if death occurs. James 1:27 says: "What God the Father considers to be pure and genuine religion is this: to take care of orphans and widows in their suffering."

If the person or their family members depend upon sex work to survive, help them find another way to make a living.

F. Assure them of God's understanding and love

It helps to know that the Bible talks about people in difficult situations that are like living with HIV/AIDS. In Psalm 38 David describes many of the emotions that people living with HIV/AIDS might feel. (If time permits, read Psalm 38.)

A person living with HIV/AIDS needs to know that God loves them. We can remind them of God's promises, such as:

- Deuteronomy 31:8: "The LORD himself will lead you and be with you. He will not fail you or abandon you, so do not lose courage or be afraid."
- Psalm 73:26: "My mind and my body may grow weak, but God is my strength; he is all I ever need."
- Isaiah 40:29: "He strengthens those who are weak and tired."

Closing   20 min

DISCUSSION

F | *(15 min) Small group. Give each group 5 minutes for activity 1. Then have a representative from each group be part of a panel that presents their plans to the large group, for 10 minutes. As facilitator, act as the host of the panel.*

1. Think about HIV-positive people in your community or church. If you do not already have a church program to serve them, together come up with a plan for how you could help them. Then select a representative from your group, to present your plan to the large group.

F | *(5 min) Small group or pairs.*

2. After reading this lesson, what is one thing you would like to start doing in your church?

Answers to quiz

1. Acquired Immune Deficiency Syndrome
2. Human Immunodeficiency Virus
3. Blood, fluids from sexual organs, and breast milk
4. Through unprotected sex
5. No. Antiretroviral drugs only reduce the growth of HIV. They do not cure it.
6. a. No, b. Yes, c. No, d. No, e. Yes, f. Yes, g. No, h. Yes
7. No
8. Blood test in a laboratory

11. Domestic abuse

This lesson produces strong emotions, and discussions can easily extend beyond the allotted time. Keep a close eye on the time.

Before you begin:

- For Section 1: Decide how you will present the story (see page 190, "Stories" in "Preparing the lessons").
- For Section 2: Get two cups for the cup illustration (See Answers to true/false exercise, number 2, last page of lesson).
- For Section 3: If needed, prepare slips of paper or index cards with Bible verses or download the Bible verses PDF.
- If you are short on time, decide if you will skip Section 4. See note in that section.

In this lesson we will:

- Define and describe domestic abuse.
- Consider what the Bible says about how we should treat family members and compare that with cultural beliefs and practices.
- Discuss how to help people trapped in abusive situations.
- Discuss how to help abusers repent and take steps toward recovery.

Section 1: Story	15 min
Section 2: What is domestic abuse?	20 min
Section 3: What do your culture and the Bible say about how we should treat family members?	25 min
Section 4: Why does domestic abuse continue?	10 min
Section 5: How can we help victims of domestic abuse?	25 min
Section 6: How can we help abusers?	5 min
Closing	5 min
Total time	**1 hour 50 minutes**

11. Domestic abuse

F | *(1 min) Introduce lesson title and objectives. Direct participants to the corresponding lesson in Healing the Wounds of Trauma.*

Section 1.   15 min

Ann leaves Joe

F | *(5 min) Large group. Present the story.*

"You need to leave him!" Mary said. She was tying a bandage on her neighbor Ann's arm after Ann's husband had beaten her yet again.

Ann had been married for three years. For the first year of their marriage, Ann and Joe were happy together. They were both Christians—Joe having come to Christ in recent years out of a troubled past. As a child, he saw his father beat his mother all the time. Problems erupted for Ann and Joe when two things happened at once: Ann gave birth to a baby boy that cried all the time, and Joe lost his job.

Joe chose to respond to these problems by going out and drinking with his friends. When he came home, Ann smelled perfume on his clothes. He also became angry more easily, especially as he had to deal with the difficulty of finding another job.

Ann tried to do things to please Joe, but whatever she did just seemed to irritate him more. He began to shout at her a lot. There was little money coming in for food, so Ann found a part-time job and someone to care for the baby, but this only seemed to make things worse. Joe kept telling her that she was a bad wife and mother.

One night, Joe came home drunk and hit her so hard that she fell against a table and broke her arm. Joe was beside himself as he took her to the hospital. He said over and over, "I didn't mean to do that! Please forgive me and don't tell the doctor!" Ann still loved Joe and thought that maybe now he would change, so she told the doctor that she had tripped and fallen outside the house.

Then for a few weeks, Joe didn't hit Ann, but his anger came out in harsh words. He said, "You're so stupid. You can't even look after the baby properly!" She began to think she should leave him for the sake of the baby, but then she thought, "How could I live without Joe? I'm so stupid. How could I earn enough money to survive? Besides, our pastor said that wives should submit to their husbands as the head of the home!" Just then, Joe came and said he was sorry for yelling at her again, and they made up. Ann lived for those brief moments.

Before long, Joe came home drunk again. The baby was crying when he walked in the door. First he hit Ann hard, and then he said, "That stupid baby!" He picked up the little boy and slapped him. The baby screamed louder. Ann grabbed the baby from his arms and ran outside. Joe followed her, yelling.

Ann banged on Mary's door. As soon as it opened she jumped inside. "Don't let Joe in!" she gasped. Mary's husband barred the door as Joe tried to bash it in. After a few minutes, he gave up and walked back to his house, kicking the neighbor's dog as he went.

Ann had finally had enough! Mary suggested she call a kind older lady in the church that she knew and find out if Ann could go and stay there for the moment. Ann agreed to that, and as the woman was happy to welcome her there and then, Mary's husband took Ann and her baby to the woman. She also suggested that she phone her pastor's wife and ask her to go and see Ann the next day, and Ann agreed to this as well.

The next morning the pastor's wife went to see Ann and they talked for a long time. The pastor's wife told Ann that she could not take responsibility to make their marriage work on her own, because Joe had broken the vows they made when they wed. He had promised to love and to cherish her, and clearly he was not doing so. She read from Ephesians 5, which showed not only that wives are to submit to their husbands, but that husbands are to love their wives, "just as Christ loved the church and gave his life for it." This was like a soothing ointment to Ann's heart.

The pastor's wife continued to meet with Ann, listening to her story and helping her see that the abuse was not her fault—and that she was not stupid! The church helped Ann and her baby find a place to live, and she was able to pay the bills by working longer hours at her job. Then one night Joe called her, and she began to waver. Should she go back to him?

DISCUSSION

F | *(5 min) Small group. Divide Questions 1–3 among the small groups. Have each group discuss Question 4. Have each group select someone to take notes and speak for the group. (If possible, have the group select a different person for each small group discussion going forward.)*

1. Why do you think Joe abused Ann?
2. Why do you think Ann stayed with Joe even though he was violent and abusive?
3. What helped Ann get out of this abusive situation?
4. How much is domestic abuse an issue in your community or family?

F | *(5 min) Large group. Get feedback. If the participants are using books, encourage them to keep them closed as much as possible for the rest of the lesson.*

Section 2.

20 min

What is domestic abuse?

F | *Mention section title. Present the sentence below.*

God calls us to treat family members with respect and kindness, but some homes are like war zones—places of domestic abuse.

F | *(10 min) Large group. Ask the group to define domestic abuse. Add content below that was not mentioned.*

Domestic abuse is a pattern of someone trying to control another family member. One person with more power asserts it over another with less power. Abuse can be directed towards elders, spouses or partners, siblings, or children. The majority of victims are females, but males can also be victims of domestic abuse. It can take many forms:

- **physical:** beating, choking, throwing things, kicking, and so on.
- **verbal:** telling the victim they are stupid, unable to do anything right, and so on.
- **emotional:** making the victim live in fear, isolating the victim from others.
- **sexual:** forcing sexual relations on the victim.
- **economic:** not allowing the victim to have money, food, education, medical help, and so on.
- **spiritual:** misusing Bible verses, teaching, and prayer to humiliate, control, or exploit the victim.

F | *Draw the cycle of abuse on the board, flip chart, or large paper. Explain it by presenting the content below the diagram. Then ask, "In the story we read, at what points was there tension? At what points was there abuse? At what points was there calm?" Then ask, "Did you see a pattern?"*

Fig. 11.1: The domestic abuse cycle

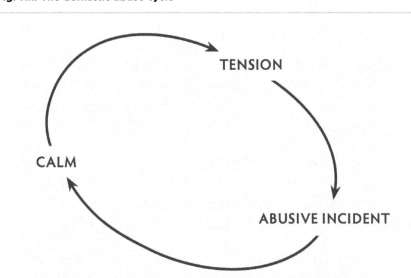

All families have conflicts, but when there is a pattern of control and manipulation, it is domestic abuse. The abuse often happens in a predictable cycle: tension, abusive incident, calm; tension, abusive incident, calm…. The cycle can happen daily, or on certain days like weekends. Over time, the victim may begin to feel unable to live without the abuser and may live for the times of calm and making up. Even if victims leave the abuser, often they return.

EXERCISE: TRUE OR FALSE?

F | *(10 min) Large group. Read these statements aloud and have each person mark down his or her response. Then go over each statement and discuss it, referring to the content*

1. Violence within the home is a private family matter.
2. Alcohol and drugs are the main causes of domestic abuse.
3. At times it can be helpful to beat family members.
4. A victim could stop the abuse if she or he really tried.
5. Often, the abuse stops without help from others.
6. Someone who is violent inside the home will also be violent outside the home.

Answers to exercise on last page of lesson.

Fig. 11.2: An abused woman

Section 3.

25 min

What does your culture and the Bible say about how we should treat family members?

F | *Mention section title.*

DISCUSSION

F | *(3 min) Large group.*

1. What are common beliefs or sayings about how family members treat each other in your culture (for example, husband-wife, parent-child)?

F | *(5 min) Small group. Divide the verses among the groups to discuss.*

2. What do these verses teach about relationships in the family?

   1 Peter 3:7   Genesis 1:26–27   Ephesians 5:21–30

   1 Corinthians 13:4–7   Colossians 3:17–21   Ephesians 4:29–32

F | *(12 min) Large group. Get feedback. Add content below that was not mentioned.*

A husband should respect his wife and treat her with understanding because she also is an equal recipient of God's gift of life. The husband's own spiritual health depends on this (1 Peter 3:7).

Both males and females are created in God's image and therefore deserve equal care (Genesis 1:26–27).

We are each to show our reverence for Christ by submitting to one another. Husband and wife have responsibilities to each other, based on the relationship between Jesus and the church. Jesus does not hurt the church in any way. Jesus gave up his life to rescue the church from death, so the husband should be willing to do the same for his wife. He should care for his wife as he cares for his own body (Ephesians 5:21–32).

A person who abuses, does not truly love (1 Corinthians 13:4–7).

Everything we do flows out of our relationship with God, including our family relationships. All family members are to relate to each other with respect, love, and kindness (Colossians 3:17–21).

As people who belong to God, our words and behaviors should be tender and compassionate. If we are harsh and insulting, we bring sorrow to God. We are to forgive, as God has forgiven us (Ephesians 4:29–32).

DISCUSSION

F | *(5 min) Large group.*

Do people in your community believe the Bible teaches us to treat family members harshly? If yes, what passages do they use and what do they say? Be sure to read the whole passage in context!

Section 4.   10 min

Why does domestic abuse continue?

F | *Mention section title. If you have already covered this content adequately in the discussion of the story, feel free to skip this section.*

DISCUSSION

F | *(5 min) Large group. After the discussion, add content below that was not mentioned.*

1. We saw in the story that there were many reasons the husband abused the wife. What were those reasons? Are there other reasons a person might abuse family members?

Abusers may:

- have grown up in a home with domestic violence and not know how to relate to family members in healthy ways.
- believe it is acceptable to beat family members. The culture or religion may teach this.
- feel powerless in their lives, but powerful when they are beating another person.
- feel jealous and insecure in their marriage, fearing their spouse will leave them if they could.
- blame their actions on others.

DISCUSSION

F | *(5 min) Large group. After the discussion, add content below the question that was not mentioned.*

2. We saw in the story that there were many reasons the wife stayed in the abusive relationship. What were those reasons? Are there other reasons an abused person might stay?

Abuse victims may:

- depend on the abuser for income and not be able to survive financially without him or her.
- believe they cannot survive emotionally on their own. The abuse humiliates them until they think they do not deserve respect.
- believe it is normal to be beaten, threatened, and insulted.
- believe it is wrong to leave their spouse.
- be afraid of the consequences of resisting the abuser.
- feel ashamed to let anyone know what is happening in their home. This is especially true if churches foster the idea that Christians should never have this problem.
- really love the abuser.
- believe they are bound to their marriage vows no matter the violence against them.

Section 5.   25 min

How can we help victims of domestic abuse?

DISCUSSION

F | *(5 min) Small group.*

1. How can victims of domestic abuse be helped? If you are a victim of domestic abuse or know of someone who has been a victim, what has been helpful?

F | *(10 min) Large group. Get feedback. Add content below that was not mentioned.*

- *Listen*: Victims need someone they can talk to, but this can be difficult because often abusers isolate their victims from contact with others.
- *Avoid marital counseling*: Don't recommend the couple see a counselor together because often abusers act kindly in front of the counselor, and then take out their rage on the victim once at home. Encourage the victim to consider individual counseling.

- *Why stay?* Ask victims, "What are the reasons you stay in the relationship?" Don't pressure them to leave but ask them about the negative things in the relationship as well as positive things. Help them recognize the cycle of abuse.
- *See effects*: Victims need to see the effects the violence is having on them and their family. If there are religious or cultural values that encourage the victim to remain in an abusive relationship, these need to be addressed.
- *Not their fault*: Help victims understand that the abuse is not their fault; it is the fault of the abuser. God sees what is happening (Psalm 10). Only the abuser can change his or her behavior.
- *Set boundaries*: Victims can decide what they will tolerate, such as, "If he hurts the children again, I will leave."
- *A plan*: They need to develop a safety plan to get out of the situation. The safest time to leave is when things are calm, rather than in the heat of a crisis. They need a place to go where the abuser cannot find them. They need practical help, such as a job and legal assistance. They may leave several times before leaving for good.
- *Healing of heart wounds*: Victims need to find healing for their heart wounds and, in due course, forgive their abusers. The trust that has been broken can only be rebuilt over time.
- *Church leaders address domestic abuse*: Pastors and ministry leaders can make the church a safer place for victims if they speak out against domestic abuse, offer practical assistance for victims, and discourage victims from staying in unsafe situations.

DISCUSSION

F | *(5 min) Small group.*

2. What has your church done to be ready to help victims of domestic abuse? What else could be done?

F | *(5 min) Large group. Get feedback. If there is not time for feedback in the large group, have groups post their answers on the wall.*

Section 6. 5 min

How can we help abusers?

F | *Mention section title. Present the sentences below.*

It is not the victim's responsibility to change the abuser's behavior. However, other people can play an important role.

DISCUSSION

F | *(5 min) Large group. After the discussion, add the content below the question that was not mentioned.*

How might someone help an abuser change?

Some ways we can help an abuser change are to:

- Help them realize that they have a problem. Often, they have deceived themselves and blame others.
- Encourage them to get professional help, if available, from a counselor with expertise in working with abusers. Have resources ready to suggest.
- Help them deal with the root causes of their problems and find healing.
- Help them identify the things that trigger their abusive behavior and develop better ways of responding.
- If they are using drugs or alcohol, help them see the need to stop. Support groups can help.
- Help them understand that repentance includes honestly admitting what they have done, making efforts to repair the damage they have caused, and working with someone who will help them change.
- Help them seek and receive God's forgiveness for what they have done.
- Don't let them pressure the victim to come back. Their behavior needs to change, and trust needs to be restored before reconciliation is possible.

Closing

5 min

F | *(5 min) Small group. Present the paragraph below, then allow time for participants to pray.*

Since domestic abuse is common, it is quite probable that there are some of you who have been or are its victims. In your small groups, take time now to pray for people who are living in abusive situations or who are still suffering the pain from having been in an abusive situation.

Answers to true/false exercise

All are false.

1. *Violence within the home is a private family matter.*

It is sin, and sin needs to be brought into the light and addressed, or it festers and grows. In the majority of countries, domestic abuse is a crime. The church is called to protect people who are mistreated and powerless.

2. *Alcohol and drugs are the main cause of domestic violence.*

People can abuse their partner without ever drinking alcohol or taking drugs, but alcohol and drugs make abuse happen more easily, like putting kerosene on charcoal to start a fire. The main cause for domestic abuse is the desire to control and intimidate others. This may be due to not experiencing healthy, loving relationships during their childhood.

F | **Cup illustration:** *As you hold a cup of water, ask a volunteer to bump your arm.*
Ask, "What caused the water to spill out of my cup?" Many will say that the cause of the spill is the person who bumped into you.

Without additional comments, hold an empty cup and ask the same volunteer to bump into you. Now ask, "Why did no water spill out this time?" Participants will most likely point out that there was no water in the cup to spill.

Say, "Exactly. Just as water cannot come out of the cup if it is not there already, neither can abusive behavior come out unless the desire to control and intimidate others is already inside of us. The Bible teaches us that what we say comes from inside of us, and not from our circumstances (Luke 6:45). Circumstances do not cause abusive behavior, but they can reveal what is in our heart."

3. *At times it can be helpful to beat family members.*

Sometimes people use force to make spouses or children obey and submit. But in Ephesians 6:4 we read, "Parents, do not treat your children in such a way as to make them angry. Instead, raise them with Christian discipline and instruction." And in Colossians 3:19 we read, "Husbands, love your wives and do not be harsh with them." Beating may result in obedience, but it is based in fear, and it makes the home a place that is not safe. To beat family members is to humiliate them and make them feel small, rather than becoming the wonderful people God created them to be.

4. *A victim could stop the abuse if she or he really tried.*

Only the abuser can stop the abuse. No one can make them stop. The abuser is responsible for his or her actions (Matthew 15:18–19).

5. *Often, abuse stops without outside intervention.*

Abusers need to face their personal problems for the abuse to stop, and most often they cannot do this without help. People do not give up power easily. Even if the physical abuse stops, the abuser can continue to control the victim without losing their temper or becoming violent, for example, clearing their throat or giving a certain look.

6. *Someone who is violent towards a partner will be violent towards others.*

Abusers know how to be very pleasant in public. Usually, it's not possible to tell an abusive person from other people. For example, there have been many cases of well-respected church leaders, well-liked by their congregation, who secretly were abusing their spouses at home.

Before you begin:

- For Section 1: Decide how you will present the story (see page 190, "Stories" in "Preparing the lessons"). Do **not** act this story out. Acting out a suicide story can be disturbing for some and may trigger painful responses.
- For Section 3: If needed, prepare slips of paper or index cards with Bible verses or download the Bible verses PDF.
- For Sections 4 and 5: Make four copies of the skit and find four participants willing to act it out. Have them practice it before the session begins. If you will read the narrator's lines, you only need three participants.
- If the theme of the skit is not appropriate for your context, adjust the text for a common cause of suicide in your area. Examples: someone who has been sexually or physically abused, a student bullied at school, a husband losing his job. You should also adjust the text to talk about suicide in the way it is discussed in your culture. For example, in the United States, people can ask direct questions like, "Have you ever thought of killing yourself?" In other countries, it is more appropriate to ask, "Have you lost all hope?"

In this lesson we will:

- Discuss the causes and effects of suicide on everyone affected by it.
- Explore examples of biblical characters who considered suicide and evaluate their responses.
- Compare the culture's understanding of and response to suicide with the Bible and mental health principles.
- Discuss how to tell how seriously someone is considering suicide and respond appropriately.
- Discuss ways to help the loved ones of those who have either attempted or died by suicide heal from the trauma of the experience.

Section 1: Story	15 min
Section 2: Why do people take their own life?	10 min
Section 3: People in the Bible who did not want to continue living	15 min
Section 4: Warning signs that someone may be considering suicide	20 min
Section 5: What can be done to help people considering suicide?	15 min
Section 6: How can we help loved ones of someone who has attempted or died by suicide?	15 min
Closing	5-10 min
Total time	**1 hour 35-40 minutes**

12. Suicide

F | *(1 min) Introduce lesson title and objectives. Direct participants to the corresponding lesson in Healing the Wounds of Trauma.*

Section 1.   15 min

Amber is gone!

F | *(5 min) Large group. Present story. Do not act this story out.*

Stephanie waited all evening for her friend Amber to come to the park as she usually did, but she never came. Since Amber's house was on her way home, Stephanie thought she would stop by and see why Amber had not come this evening.

As she neared Amber's home, she saw many cars there. She almost walked on but decided to at least tell Amber good night. As she neared the front door, she could hear people crying inside.

She knocked gently on the screen door. Amber's brother opened the door for her and as she stepped inside, Amber's grandmother hugged her and cried even harder. "My Amber is gone!" she cried. "Amber is gone!" The shock went through Stephanie's body like a lightning bolt and she wept for a long time with the grandmother. Then she heard the story. Amber had taken her own life by overdosing herself with prescription painkillers. It seemed so unreal.

Stephanie attended the funeral, but it was a blur. In the weeks that followed, she felt as if life didn't have much meaning. She lost her appetite. Her grades dropped. Although she had been friends before with some of Amber's brothers and sisters, now she avoided the whole family. She couldn't fall asleep, and when she did, she often had nightmares. But one night, she dreamed that Amber came and told her how much she loved her.

One day, her own grandmother asked her to sit with her under the tree in the backyard. After several minutes of silence, she started to stroke Stephanie's hair. "Stephanie," she began, "Your friend has been gone a while. At first, I was afraid that you might want to join her, but now I'm afraid that you are like the dead while you are still living. When are you going to come back?" She held Stephanie's thin, fragile wrist in her old hands.

"Why, Grandma? Why did she do that? I didn't know she felt that way. I wasn't there for her. I couldn't even save my friend, Grandma!" Grandma said, "Let your tears out, dear. We may never know why Amber did it. It wasn't your fault. Amber made her choice, and we make ours." Stephanie cried and cried, like something had broken open inside her. Grandma said, "Anytime you want to, just come here."

Stephanie spent a lot of time at her grandma's. They talked together and cried together. They cooked together and played games together. Little by little, Stephanie began to laugh again. After a couple years had passed, whenever she thought about Amber, Stephanie remembered what a wonderful friend she had been rather than thinking first about how she died.

DISCUSSION

F | (5 min) Small group. Assign one question per small group or pair. Or have each group answer both—in that case you will need more than 5 minutes. Have each group select someone to take notes and speak for the group. (If possible, have the group select a different person for each small group discussion going forward.)

1. How did Amber's suicide affect Stephanie?
2. Do you know anyone who has taken his or her life or attempted suicide? What effect did it have on their loved ones?

F | (5 min) Large group. Get feedback. If the participants are using books, encourage them to keep them closed as much as possible for the rest of the lesson.

Section 2. 10 min

Why do people take their own life?

F | (2 min) Mention section title. Present the content below.

Suicide is taking one's own life intentionally. It happens in all societies and by all kinds of people: young and old, men and women.

In some cases, it may be unclear whether a suicide was intentional or accidental, such as when a person overdoses on drugs or alcohol and dies.

It is common to say "commit suicide," but in some cultures it is more considerate to say "die by suicide" or "take his/her own life."

DISCUSSION

F | (8 min) Large group. After the discussion, add content below the question that was not mentioned.

Why do people take their own life?

Every case is different, but:
- Some may have lost all hope.
- Some may be in great emotional pain, even though they may seem to be happy and are active with friends and family.
- Some may be hiding something they feel is so shameful they don't dare tell anyone. They feel suicide is the only response to shame.
- Some are convinced their loved ones would be better off without them.
- Some are very angry and react by taking their own life.
- Others take their own life to punish loved ones.
- They may have a family member or friend who has attempted or died by suicide and be tempted to follow their example.
- Some may be abused or bullied by others. Suicide may feel like the only way out.

Section 3.

People in the Bible who did not want to continue living

F | *Mention section title, then introduce the discussion question.*

DISCUSSION

F | *(5 min) Small group. Divide the Bible passages among the small groups.*

Read one of the passages below about people in the Bible. Discuss what you know about the main characters. What might they have been feeling? What did they do?

Saul and his armor bearer (1 Samuel 31:1–5)

Ahithophel (2 Samuel 17:1–7, 14, 23)

Elijah (1 Kings 19:1–4)

Job (Job 3:11–14)

Jonah (Jonah 4:1–3)

Philippian jailer (Acts 16:25–28)

F | *(10 min) Large group. Get feedback. Add content below that was not mentioned.*

Examples of people who died by suicide:

- Saul asked his armor bearer to help kill him in order to avoid pain and shame. Then the armor bearer took his own life, too.
- Ahithophel hanged himself when his advice was not followed. He may have felt ashamed and hopeless.

Examples of those who wanted to die but did not kill themselves:

- Elijah felt despair and prayed for God to take him.
- Job felt hopeless and cursed the day he was born.
- Jonah was angry with God and wanted to die.

Example of someone who was about to kill himself, but someone stopped him: The Philippian jailer.

Many people in the Bible were so desperate they wanted to die, including people of great faith. Elijah, Job, and Jonah honestly expressed their wish to die to God (1 Kings 19:1–4; Job 3:11–14; Jonah 4:1–3). This did not stop God from loving them. We know that nothing can separate us from God's love. The apostle Paul writes:

> *For I am certain that nothing can separate us from his love: neither death nor life, neither angels nor other heavenly rulers or powers, neither the present nor the future, neither the world above nor the world below—there is nothing in all creation that will ever be able to separate us from the love of God which is ours through Christ Jesus our Lord.* (Romans 8:38–39)

We know that having suicidal feelings or taking one's life does not stop God from loving us.

Section 4.

20 min

12

Warning signs that someone may be considering suicide

F (15 min) Mention section title. Have four participants act out Scenes 1 and 2 of the skit about assessing the risk of suicide (Scene 3 is in Section 5).

Skit: A pregnant student

Scene 1: Missing the signs

Narrator: While attending boarding school, Josephine suddenly began to have trouble with her studies. She started skipping class and staying in her room. When she came to meals, she did not finish her food or talk to anyone. After a week, her friend Pauline visited her in her room.

Pauline (P): (Knock on the door, entering room) I came to see why you are so quiet. Things cannot be that bad.

Josephine (J): Well, they are really bad. (Sigh)

P: Well, what are you going to do about it?

J: (Shrug of shoulders, head looking down) I don't know.

P: You cannot stay here in your room all the time. Your grades will drop.

J: They already are bad; I just am not able to concentrate.

P: I can help you with that. What do you want to study first?

J: (Shifting in her chair away from Pauline) I don't know; I just feel awful.

P: You probably just need some help with your studies. Let's go and study together. First though, let's make sure we eat dinner.

J: (Sitting more slumped in chair) No, I don't think so. It doesn't seem worth it to try anymore. I feel like giving up.

P: (Becoming a little more dramatic, lifting her arms, standing up) You can't say that, Josephine. We have a God who cares for us and loves us. We need to hope in him; otherwise we are being weak in our faith. Let me pray for you.

J: (Has no choice but to let Pauline hold her hands to pray) Okay, though I don't know if it will help. I have been praying and I have only felt worse. I do not have hope.

P: (Prays) Dear God, help Josephine know you care for her. Help her to feel better and to be obedient by focusing more on her school work. Amen. Feel better?

J: (Shrug of shoulders) I'm not sure.

P: (Gets up to leave) In the morning, with a good night's sleep, I am sure you will feel better. See you in class tomorrow.

J: (Does not look up) Bye.

DISCUSSION

F | (5 min) Large group. Discuss the questions. For Question 2, be sure to note the following warning signs of Josephine: "I am just not able to concentrate." "I feel like giving up." "I do not have hope."

1. What do you think about the way Pauline responded to Josephine?
2. What warning signs did Pauline miss?

F | (2 min) Continue with scene 2 of the skit.

Scene 2: Paying attention to the signs

Narrator: A few days later, another friend, Sarah, visited Josephine.

Sarah (S):   (Knock on the door, entering room) Hello Josephine, I came to see why you are so quiet and have spent so much time alone in your room. Is there something wrong?

Josephine (J): (Sighs, looks up a little) I just have not been feeling well.

S: When was the last time you ate?

J: Yesterday.

S: (Sits down and looks at Josephine) What happened?

J: (Looking down) Well, I am not sure what to say.

S: It's okay. Begin where you can. I am concerned about you.

J: Thank you, but I think I will be okay.

S: I'm not so sure. You have been so quiet and missing classes. This is not like you. Tell me what has happened.

J: It is hard to talk about.

S: What happened first?

J: (Looking up just briefly) Do you remember Dan?

S: Yes, he came to visit with the boys from the other boarding school nearby.

J: (Becomes more quiet, looks down)

S: Something happened during the visit with Dan?

J: (Nods her head yes, looks more sad)

S: Josephine, I can see that you are upset, you can talk to me.

J: (Shakes her head no) I don't think I can talk to anyone. It is all my fault. My father—you know he's a pastor; he will never accept me. There is no hope for me.

> F | Say, "At this point you may be tempted to try to learn more about what has happened. However, Josephine spoke of losing hope. If someone begins to talk about losing hope, not being around anymore, trying to escape, or ending their life, begin to focus on assessing the risk for suicide, not on getting more details. Not everyone will say, 'I have lost all hope' or 'I want to end it all,' so if you notice a significant change in behavior, you can ask the person, 'Have you lost all hope?'"

DISCUSSION

> F | (5 min) Large group. After discussing the questions, add content below the questions that was not mentioned.

1. How was Sarah's response to Josephine different than Pauline's response?
2. What were the warning signs that Josephine was considering suicide?
3. What other signs have you noticed when someone is considering suicide?

Possible warning signs:

- They may become withdrawn and isolate themselves from others.
- They may talk about wanting to die or say things like, "What's the point of living?" or "Soon you won't have to worry about me!"
- They may give away things that are very important to them.
- They may change suddenly from being depressed to being very happy for no obvious reason.
- They may neglect taking care of themselves.

Not everyone considering suicide gives warning signs like this, but if they do, take them seriously!

Section 5. 15 min

How can we help people considering suicide?

> F | Mention section title. Continue with scene 3 of the skit.

Scene 3: Responding in a helpful way

Sarah (S): What do you mean that there is no hope for you?

Josephine (J): I think I would rather not be here anymore. My life is ruined.

S: Ruined? Have you thought of ending your life? [Or, "Have you thought about doing something so that you won't have to live with this anymore?"]

J: (Sits quietly, nods her head yes) You don't understand. My family will not accept me. I just found out I'm pregnant. There is no way out.

S: Have you thought about how you would end your life? [Or, "Have you decided to do what you've been thinking about?"]

J: Yes.

S: Do you have a plan?

> F *Pause and say, "Asking more specific questions helps you learn if the person's thoughts about suicide have become more than just thoughts. If you learn that the thoughts also include a plan and a way to carry out that plan, there is greater risk for suicide."*

J: I can overdose by taking pills.

S: Do you have the pills here in your room?

J: (Nod of the head, yes)

S: Can you give them to me? Or can you show me where they are?

J: But, you don't understand. What else can I do?

S: (Softly) Josephine, I want to help you find a different answer to this problem. I will be here with you. Please show me where the pills are.

J: (Gets the pills and gives them to Sarah.)

S: I would like to stay here with you tonight. Is that okay? I want to make sure that you are safe.

J: (Nods her head) Yes.

S: I am here for you. Together we will figure out what to do. Let's get some dinner, and after a good night's sleep we can also think about other things that we can do to help you feel better.

J: Okay.

S: We can also think of other people who can help you. Maybe we can find a counselor. Would that be okay?

J: (Softly) I think so.

DISCUSSION

> F *(5 min) Small group. Divide the questions among the groups.*

1. What did you see in the skit that can be done to help people considering suicide?
2. What else can be done to help people considering suicide?

> F *(10 min) Large group. Get feedback. Add content below that was not mentioned.*

Talk about it:
- Do not avoid talking about suicide for fear of offending them or of putting the idea into their minds.
- Find out how serious they are. Have they made a plan? Have they prepared? Have they practiced? Have they thought through how this will affect others?
- Do not preach at them or tell them what to do. Instead, ask questions that will help them express how they are feeling. Tears are good. Help them find ways to release their pain and express their anger.

Keep them safe:
- If they are serious about attempting suicide, remove any means of doing so from their environment, such as medicines, ropes, guns, and so forth.
- Don't leave them alone. Be with them or find someone else to be with them.

Build hope:

- Ask them to imagine their situation being just a little bit better. What would have changed?
- Explore what has kept them from committing suicide so far. Try to build hope on those ideas. For example, if a mother is concerned about the future of her child, discuss how much her child needs her.
- Find out what they have already tried to overcome their problems and help them think about what else they could try.
- Assure them that others have been in similar situations and there is a way out other than death.

Help them find additional support:

- Find out if there is a suicide hotline in their community and, if so, help them call it.
- Help them connect with others. Healing comes as they tell their story and reconnect with others. Even if they have professional help, they will still need the support of friends and loved ones.
- Medications for depression may help. If they are already on medication, encourage them to continue taking it.
- Find a professional counselor to help them.
- If there are no suicide prevention programs in your community, consider working with others to organize one. Help schools become aware that when a student attempts or dies by suicide, other students may be tempted to follow their example.

Section 6.   15 min

How can we help loved ones of someone who has attempted or died by suicide?

F | *(1 min) Mention section title. Present the paragraph below.*

All death and loss is painful, but when someone dies by suicide, the grief of loved ones is especially painful. Their lives will be marked "before the suicide" and "after the suicide." If a person attempts suicide but does not succeed, the effect on his or her loved ones will still be profound. Their lives will be changed.

DISCUSSION

F | *(5 min) Large group. After the discussion, add content below the question that was not mentioned.*

1. How do you think the loved ones of someone who has attempted or died by suicide may feel?

They may feel:

- guilty that they did not see the warning signs.
- guilty that they were not able to stop the person.

- angry with the person for taking their life (or trying to do so).
- stuck in their grieving process, which may be complicated and prolonged.
- ashamed, and the community may add to their shame. For example, in some communities, people who take their own life are not buried in the normal way.
- that they need to understand why the suicide happened or why the person attempted suicide.
- afraid more bad things will happen or that the person will attempt suicide again.
- unable to trust others again, particularly the person who attempted suicide.
- especially distressed if their religious tradition teaches that suicide is an unforgivable sin
- betrayed, wondering why the person did not share his or her pain
- responsible for the suicide

Children especially may think it is their fault. The lesson on children (Lesson 8) may help adults know how to help a child work through the loss of someone by suicide.

DISCUSSION

F | *(5 min) Small group. Divide the questions among the small groups.*

1. When a person in your community dies by suicide, what ways do people treat his or her loved ones that are helpful? What ways are unhelpful?
2. How can you help the loved ones of someone who has died by suicide? If someone you loved died by suicide, what has helped you?

F | *(5 min) Large group. Get feedback. Add content below that was not mentioned.* **Note:** *The responsibility of taking one's own life ultimately lies with that person. This is true even if others said or did things that may have contributed to the hopelessness that person felt. Other factors can also have an effect on their emotional state and ability to cope, such as a culture of perfection in academics, bullying, influences from social media, and expectations of what it means to be a man or woman.*

Ways to help the loved ones of someone who has died by suicide:
- Help with physical needs.
- Provide normal funeral services for those who die by suicide. If the suicide was in the past and there was no funeral, have a ceremony or time of remembrance for the person.
- Spend time with them.
- Talk about suicide openly without shaming them.
- Listen to them. Use the three listening questions from the healing lesson.
- Help them realize they are not responsible for what happened.
- Help them accept that they may never understand why the person did it. There are no simple answers for why a person takes his or her own life.
- Help them remember the good things about the person's life, not only the way he or she died.

Closing

F | *(5–10 min) Choose one or more of the options, depending on the time available.*

1. Pray for those in your community affected by suicide.
2. Draw or create an image, a word art (as in the Suffering lesson), or a collage of pictures and words from magazines and/or textiles that reminds you of comfort and hope. In pairs, share as much as you would like and pray for one another.
3. Discuss the following questions, in pairs:
   - Have you ever known someone who wanted to end their life? How did you feel about them wanting to end their life? What did you do?
   - Have you ever been so discouraged or frustrated that you wanted to die? What was that like for you? What helped you overcome that feeling?
4. What is the most important thing you want to remember from this lesson?

12

13. Addictions

Before you begin:

- For Section 1: Decide how you will present the story (see page 190, "Stories" in "Preparing the lessons").
- For Section 4: If needed, prepare slips of paper or index cards with Bible verses or download the Bible verses PDF.
- For Section 5: Find two participants who are willing to act out the "Addictions role-play" skit. Have them practice it before the session begins.
- Decide whether you will use section 6A ("How can you help family members?") or 6B ("How has addiction impacted your life?"), depending upon the participants in your group.
- Decide which Closing exercises you will use.
- Consider spending two sessions on this lesson according to the needs of your group. This would allow for more discussion and doing more of the options.

In this lesson we will:

- Define an addiction.
- Discuss how people become and stay addicted.
- Gain wisdom from the Bible that can help people who are addicted.
- Discover how to respond appropriately to someone with an addiction according to the stage they have reached in wanting to recover.
- Discuss how to help family and friends of a person with an addiction.

Section 1: Story	15 min
Section 2: What is an addiction?	5 min
Section 3: Why are people addicted?	30 min
Section 4: What wisdom from the Bible can help people who are addicted?	20 min
Section 5: How can we help people with an addiction?	15 min
Section 6: How can we help family members of a person with an addiction?	30 min
Closing	5–15 min
Total time	**2 hours – 2 hours 10 minutes**

13. Addictions

F | *(1 min) Introduce lesson title and objectives. Direct participants to the corresponding lesson in Healing the Wounds of Trauma. Present the sentence below.*

This lesson is included because trauma can lead to addictions, and addictions often cause trauma to both the addicted and those around them.

Section 1.

15 min

Just one more

F | *(5 min) Large group. Present the story.*

"Just one more beer," David thought as he sat with his friends from work. They came to this local bar every Friday after work. His wife Michelle had asked him to be home by 6 p.m. since their twelve-year-old son Mike was going to play in his first football game with his school's team. "I'll just go directly to the school," David told himself. "Michelle knows how hard I work. It will be okay." But he missed the game.

Five years later, his son, now seventeen, was proudly playing in the national championship game. Mike knew it was pointless to look around for his father. Too many years and too many games had passed for him to expect David to be there for him. "Why even give him a thought?" said Mike to himself as he scored the goal that brought victory to his school.

After the game, Mike and Michelle went home to find David asleep in the sitting room. Several empty beer bottles were scattered on the floor. Mike went directly to his room while his mother began to pick up the bottles. The slam of his bedroom door awakened his father.

Shortly afterward, he heard his parents going over the same argument he had heard for years. "You knew tonight was the national championship! How could you have missed the game?"

"Michelle, I'm sorry. I thought I could take a quick nap and I just lost track of time," said David.

"What about these bottles?" yelled Michelle. "You promised me you would stop drinking. And it's been a month since you last had a drink."

"I know, Michelle, but you know how hard my work can be," David said. "I needed to relax. I only bought four bottles. I had every intention of being at the game. I won't let it happen again." David yelled the last sentence because Michelle had already left and slammed her own bedroom door.

DISCUSSION

F | *(5 min) Small group. Divide the questions among the small groups or pairs to discuss. Have each group select someone to take notes and speak for the group. (If possible, have the group select a different person for each small group discussion going forward.)*

1. What was David's problem?
2. What effect did his problem have on Michelle? On Mike?

F | *(5 min) Large group. Get feedback. If the participants are using books, encourage them to keep them closed as much as possible for the rest of the lesson.*

Section 2.   **5 min**

What is an addiction?

DISCUSSION

F | *(4 min) Large group. After discussing, add content below the question that was not mentioned.*

1. What is an addiction?

An addiction is an ongoing pattern of using a substance or an activity to make people feel good or help them face life. It is not easily stopped, and in the end it causes harm. An addiction differs from a habit in the following ways:
- People crave it and depend on it to face life.
- It makes them feel better, or at least keeps them from feeling pain. But when the good feeling goes away, they miss it, so they repeat the behavior again. This goes on over and over. Eventually they become unable to stop the behavior.
- As time goes on, they need to do more and more of their addictive behavior to get the same good feeling. Eventually the good feeling goes away, and people do the addiction to avoid the bad feelings that would happen if they tried to stop.
- They rely on the addictive behavior more and more and sacrifice other things to continue it.
- For chemical addictions like drugs and alcohol, the body and brain start to depend on the substance. Without it, people become physically sick. Even non-chemical addictions like sex, pornography, gambling, and gaming also affect the brain and body.
- Addictions thrive in isolation and secrecy.
- Eventually addictions destroy people's lives: their health, their families, their friendships, their jobs, and their roles in the community.

F | *(1 min) Large group. After discussing, add content below that was not mentioned.*

2. What are some things people can be addicted to?

Common addictions include alcohol, tobacco, drugs, pornography, sex, gambling, video games, social media, cell phone use, shopping, eating too much, extreme dieting, running or other exercise, and even work.

People can be addicted to things that are normally good but become harmful when they take over their life.

Section 3.

30 min

13

Why are people addicted?

DISCUSSION

F | *(5 min) Small group.*

1. Why do you think people become addicted?

F | *(5 min) Large group. Get feedback. Then add content below that was not mentioned.*

- *Social reasons:* They are with others who drink (or gamble, and so on) and they want to be accepted. They need the substance to feel relaxed with other people. Family members may have an addiction, such as drinking or pornography, that influences others in the family.
- *Personal reasons:* (1) They begin doing something because they enjoy it but then cannot control it. (2) The addiction numbs them from feeling the wounds of their heart. (3) The addiction may be a way of coping with stress or problems.
- *Personality and inherited traits:* Some people are much more likely than others to become addicted.
- *Early exposure:* Being exposed to an addictive substance or activity at an early age increases the likelihood of an addiction.
- *Kind of substance:* Certain substances and methods of use increase the likelihood of addiction. For example, drugs that are injected or smoked reach the brain within seconds.

Having one or more of these reasons to become addicted does not mean someone *will* become addicted, but it does mean it is more likely.

DISCUSSION

F | *(5 min) Small groups or pairs.*

2. Why don't people with an addiction just stop?

F | *(5 min) Large group. Get feedback. Then add content below that was not mentioned.*

- The addiction may have changed their brain and the way it functions.
- Their bodies may crave the addiction, making it painful to stop.
- They enjoy what they are doing or they think they have a right to do it.
- They are deceived and have developed habits of lying and manipulating people to get what they want.
- They think of themselves as an addict. They have lost hope that they will be able to change.
- The addiction keeps them from feeling the pain of problems they do not want to face.

F | *(10 min) Draw the cycle of addiction on the board, flip chart, or large paper. As you draw, define each stage, then ask, "Where in the story did we see this stage?"*

Fig. 13.2: The cycle of addiction

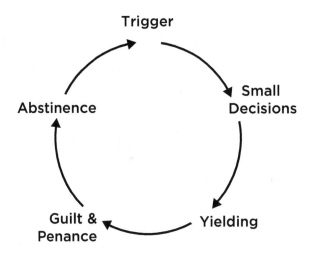

People who struggle with addictions often get trapped in a cycle. They do not always recognize the cycle or know how to stop it.

1. *Trigger:* A trigger is anything that starts the desire to engage in addictive behavior. It may include painful or positive emotions, certain thoughts or memories, stress, fatigue, certain smells, sights, or sounds. It may even happen after a person celebrates how long they have abstained from an addiction.

2. *Small decisions:* They do something really small that opens the door to the addiction again. They feel they can withstand the temptation, or that they deserve this little thing. For example, watching television, walking past a bar or past a street corner where they previously used or bought drugs, not being honest about what they are feeling.
3. *Yielding to the desire:* They yield to the addiction again and it takes over.
4. *Guilt and penance:* They feel badly and try to do good things to make up for yielding to the temptation. They also may feel shame, feeling that something is wrong with who they are.
5. *Abstinence:* They start the cycle again.

It is possible for a person with an addiction to resist and not give in to an addictive behavior. God can help them so that their desires no longer master them. God can also give them hope that one day they will be free. They will also need help from other people.

Section 4.

What wisdom from the Bible can help people who are addicted?

F | *(1 min) Present content below.*

The word "addiction" is not in the Bible. But we find there much teaching about desires, behaviors, thoughts, and temptations, all of which are involved in an addiction.

DISCUSSION

F | *(5 min) Small group. Read the question, then distribute one or two of the verses to each group or pair, to read aloud in their group and discuss.*

How do the following verses address addiction?

James 1:14–15	Romans 6:6–7, 12–13	Ephesians 4:22–24
Hebrews 4:15–16	1 Corinthians 10:13	Ecclesiastes 4:9–12

F | *(14 min) Large group. Get feedback, then add content below that was not mentioned.*

The root of temptation is not the addictive substance (or behavior). Rather it is our desire for something that we mistakenly believe the substance will provide. As we continue to try to satisfy the desire with the substance, it can lead to an addiction. Once an addiction is formed, it is very difficult to stop (James 1:14–15).

Through a relationship with Jesus, the person we once were is counted as dead, and we are set free from sin's power. This encourages us to surrender ourselves fully to God, not to the desires of our old self (Romans 6:6–7, 12–13).

As Christians we have been given a new nature. The Holy Spirit can give us new thoughts and attitudes that are consistent with this nature. We need to throw away the patterns of behavior from our old nature, like lying and lust (Ephesians 4:22–24 NLT).

Jesus does not condemn us for our weaknesses but feels sympathy for us. He understands what it is like to be tempted. When we are tempted, he will help us if we ask him (Hebrews 4:15–16).

God can help us resist temptations to addictive behaviors. He will ensure there is a way out and will show us how to endure the struggle (1 Corinthians 10:13).

It is much harder to resist temptation on our own. We are much stronger when we have the support of other people (Ecclesiastes 4:9–12).

Section 5.   15 min

How can we help people with an addiction?

F | *(1 min) Present the paragraph below. Draw the stages diagram.*

People go through stages in their willingness to deal with their addiction, and each stage requires a different response from someone who wants to help them. It is not helpful to preach to people with an addiction or try to solve their problems for them. They need to decide for themselves that they want to stop.

Fig. 13.3: The stages of addiction

STAGE 1		STAGE 2		STAGE 3		STAGE 4
I don't have a problem	>	Maybe I do have a problem	>	I have a problem; I'm stopping	>	Oh no! I did it again!

F | *(14 min) Ask the two participants who have rehearsed the Addictions role-play skit to act it out for the large group. Introduce the skit by saying, "This skit will help us know how to respond to people at different stages of dealing with their addiction. The conversations are put together from responses that might be helpful over a period of time. It would be rare for a full conversation to happen like this."*

Name each stage, then cue the "actors" to act out the stage. Pause the skit after each stage to discuss each response, as suggested below, or present the entire skit, then discuss all four responses.

Skit: Addictions role-play

A = Person with an addiction. F = Friend

Stage 1: "I don't really have a problem" (Not ready)

F: Hi Joe, how are you?
A: Fine. Everything is going okay.

F: Really? You look pretty worn out. I heard about the party this weekend.

A: That was great! I only remember some of it, but it was fun!

F: Joe, I'm concerned about you. It seems like you've been doing this every weekend for a while. I think …

A: (interrupting) No big deal. Things are fine. See you later?

F: Hear me out. I want you to know why I'm concerned about your drinking. I'm scared for how far it's going—like when you black out. It's also affecting your work and your family, and I know you care about them.

A: Really, there's nothing to worry about. Bye!

> F | *Ask, "How did the friend respond at stage 1?" Get feedback. Add content below if it was not mentioned.*

Helpful responses at stage 1: Help them think about where their lifestyle will lead and if this is what they really want.

Stage 2: "Maybe I do have a problem" (Getting ready)

F: Hey, Joe, how you doing?

A: Uh, okay, I guess.

F: What's going on?

A: Nothing really. I mean, this morning I woke up in a strange place and I can't remember what happened last night. I feel terrible today. It's kind of scary.

F: Yes, that does sound frightening.

A: Maybe I need to slow down a bit. Maybe not drink for a little while.

F: It'll be hard, but it sounds like a good idea. How do you think it would help?

A: Well, I wouldn't be hung over every weekend, and I'd be able to get to work on time. I probably wouldn't have so many fights at home.

F: That sounds really positive. And no more blackouts! Remember, I'm here for you. Give me a call anytime you're tempted to drink.

> F | *Ask, "How did the friend respond at stage 2?" Get feedback. Add content below if it was not mentioned.*

Helpful responses at stage 2: Help them think of the benefits and difficulties of giving up their addiction.

Stage 3: "I have a problem. I'm stopping" (Ready)

F: Joe, how are things?

A: Not good. You know I told you I was thinking of slowing down on the drinking?

F: Yeah, I remember that.

A: Well, I've tried slowing down, but it's not working. I'm out of control. I want to stop now, and I need help.

F: Thanks for telling me. This sounds really hard, but I want to help. Let's go have coffee … Why do you think you started in the first place?

A: I don't know. I was in high school, and my dad left my mom, and I was so angry, and then my friends, well, they drank pretty heavily.

F: So last week, what happened when you started drinking again? What was going on?

A: It was right after I had a fight with my dad. I was so angry I didn't know what to do.

F: Huh. Maybe you drink when you're angry and confused?

A: You know, that's true.

F: A friend of mine, Sally, got over an addiction. She said that when the craving hit, she waited ten minutes, tried to understand what she was feeling, and then did something to resist the temptation. Is there something good you can do when you start wanting a drink? I wonder if we could make a list.

A: Okay, well I could go running. Or take a walk. That usually makes me feel good. Or maybe, um, I could call you! I should skip television—all those beer ads!

F: That's a good start! Maybe we can find a support group, too. Would you like to meet Sally?

A: Sure. Good idea. That might help.

> F | *Ask, "How did the friend respond at stage 3?" Get feedback. Add content below if it was not mentioned.*

Helpful responses at stage 3: Praise the steps they are taking to stop their addiction, even the small steps. Encourage them often. Help them:

1. Pay attention to the roots of their addiction:
   - Begin to pay attention to their desires, thoughts, and feelings. Explore why the addiction started in the first place.
   - Address the wounds of their hearts and bring their pain to Christ for healing.
   - Ask God and others to forgive them for the problems they have brought about, and then accept the full forgiveness Christ has promised.

2. Establish new habits:
   - Pause when tempted and ask, "Am I hungry? Am I angry? Am I lonely? Am I tired?" This gives them a chance to evaluate why they are tempted. (In English, this spells "HALT": Hungry, Angry, Lonely, Tired.)
   - Avoid situations and places where they have yielded to their addiction in the past. For example, if they went to a bar with friends thinking they would order a soft drink but ended up drunk, they should avoid places where alcohol is prominent. Or if they are addicted to gaming, set bedtime routines to avoid gaming through the night.
   - Have a plan for what to do whenever they think of giving into the addiction. Often they are able to resist if they wait, get involved in an alternate activity or talk with someone who understands their craving.
   - Replace the addiction with something good (Luke 11:24–26).
   - Identify sources of tension and learn new ways to relax.

3. Find a support network:
   - Encourage them to spend more time with other people than spending time alone. When they are tempted, they need to be with other people who are not addicted.
   - Find someone who has recovered from a similar addiction whom they can call for help and report on their recovery progress.

- Connect with a local addiction recovery support group. Normally people will not recover from an addiction without support from others.
- Depending on the type of addiction, get medical help to support them in the recovery process.

Stage 4: "Oh no! I did it again!" (Falling back)

F: (concerned) Hi Joe, are you doing okay?

A: I blew it! I was doing so well! Then last night I got in a fight with my brother. I was so upset that I went to the bar and got drunk. I can't believe it.

F: I remember you said that you used to drink when you felt angry.

A: Yeah, and I had stopped drinking for five months! What am I going to do now?

F: You know, this is a normal part of recovery. It doesn't mean it's over. Today is the next step. Jesus still loves you and is walking with you on this journey. I am too. If you get angry with your brother again, please call me on the phone, okay?

> F Ask, "How did the friend respond at stage 4?" Get feedback. Add content below if it was not mentioned.

Helpful responses at stage 4:

- Remind them that falling back is a common part of the recovery process.
- Give more support so that they know that even though they have fallen, they can get up on their feet again (Psalm 37:23–24).
- Assure them that their behavior doesn't change God's love for them (Romans 5:8).

Section 6A. How can we help family members of a person with an addiction?

30 min

DISCUSSION

> F (3 min) Large group. After the discussion, add content below the question that was not mentioned.

1. How might family and friends of someone with an addiction feel?

Family members and friends of someone with an addiction may feel angry, betrayed, trapped, deceitful (due to keeping the person's secrets), frightened, anxious, helpless, hopeless, desperate, and resentful.

DISCUSSION

> F (5 min) Small groups or pairs.

2. How can we help the family members or other loved ones of a person with an addiction?

> F (12 min) Large group. Get feedback, then add content below that was not mentioned.

We can help family members or other loved ones:

- Realize how much the addictive behavior is affecting their lives and that their situation is not normal.
- Identify and heal from the heart wounds they may have experienced as a result of the person's addictions (for example, physical or emotional abuse).
- Address the challenges they face around the addiction, such as the feelings they are experiencing, differences of opinion on how to respond, financial strain due to rescuing the person, and so forth.
- Take responsibility for their own decisions and hold the person responsible for his or her decisions, allowing him or her to face the consequences.
- Talk to the person about the situation, cautiously and at the right time. This is difficult, so they may need help from other people. Most often, people with an addiction want to cover over the problem. They may feel too ashamed to talk about it.
- Adjust to life after the person recovers. Family members and friends may feel they have lost part of their identity and purpose in life after someone recovers. They may feel angry if people congratulate the person with an addiction for recovering and do not recognize how much the family has suffered through the years. They also may become aware for the first time of other problems they have that were hidden.

DISCUSSION

F | *(10 min) Discuss the questions in the large group or in groups of two or three, according to the amount of time you have.*

3. Imagine you are living with a person who is addicted. Discuss these questions.
   - What can you actually change?
   - How can you take care of yourself?
   - What things might you do, intending to help the person with an addiction stop, that actually help him or her continue, for example, covering up what is happening?

Section 6B. How has your addiction impacted your life? (For participants struggling with an addiction)   30 min

DISCUSSION

F | *(5 min) Small group.*

1. How has your addiction impacted your life?
2. How has your addiction impacted your family or significant others in your life?

F | *(5 min) Large group. Get feedback.*

DISCUSSION IN PAIRS

F | *(5 min) Pairs.*

1. When did you start the addictive behavior?
2. How did your addictive behavior change over time?
3. What is it like now?

TIMELINE ACTIVITY

F | *(10 min) Read the activity instructions, then have participants work on this individually.*

Draw a timeline. Indicate when you became addicted to the various things you are or were addicted to. Then consider the following questions.

1. For anything to which you are actively addicted right now, what will your addiction look like in six months if it goes unchecked? In one year? In five years?
2. When you look back at the age you started doing the addiction, what happened in your life before that age? Draw a picture or write out what you remember.
3. Of the causes of addictions listed in Section 3, which one(s) do you think contributed to your addiction? Was there a heart wound that you were trying to cope with through your addiction?

F | *Encourage participants to bring their pain to Jesus when the healing group does this lesson.*

DISCUSSION

F | *(5 min) Small group.*

1. Looking back at Section 5, at what stage in the addiction process are you?
2. What would going to the next stage look like?

Closing   **5–15 min**

F | *Choose between options 1–3 according to the time you have. Give participants time to answer the "one thing you want to remember" question.*

Option 1: Community readiness

DISCUSSION

F | *(5 min) Large group.*

What assistance is available in your community or church for those who want to stop an addiction or who are living with someone with an addiction?

Option 2: For those helping someone with an addiction

DISCUSSION IN PAIRS

> F | *(10 min) Pairs. Have the pairs choose from the two questions. Encourage them to share as much as they are comfortable with and then pray for each other. Close with the Serenity Prayer.*

1. Have you ever been in relationship with someone with an addiction? Are you in that situation right now? What has that been like for you?
2. Draw the addiction cycle (Section 3) of someone you care about, whom you would like God to help you assist. Draw pictures, words, or symbols for what is happening at each stage. Which part of the cycle seems the most difficult for them to break?

Pray for each other. Consider praying the Serenity Prayer, which has helped many people struggling with an addiction:

> *God, grant me the serenity to accept the things I cannot change, courage to change the things I can, and wisdom to know the difference.*

Option 3: For people struggling with an addiction

ART ACTIVITY

> F | *(15 min) Read the activity instructions and give participants 7–8 minutes to reflect and draw. Give them 7–8 minutes to share in pairs, then pray for each other. Close with the Serenity Prayer.*

Reflect on a cycle of unhealthy behavior which you find yourself repeating. Draw the cycle of addiction (Section 3), with that behavior represented in some way in the center. Draw pictures, words, or symbols for each part of the cycle in which you feel trapped.

1. Have you ever suffered from addiction? Are you addicted to something right now? Share as much as you are comfortable sharing.
2. What are ways in which you can stop the cycle?
3. Which part of the cycle is the most difficult for you to break?
4. What can you do to seek God's help to recover from addiction?

Consider praying the Serenity Prayer, which has helped many people struggling with an addiction:

> *God, grant me the serenity to accept the things I cannot change, courage to change the things I can, and wisdom to know the difference.*

What is one thing you want to remember from this lesson?

14. Caring for the caregiver

Before you begin:

- For Section 1: Decide how you will present the story (see page 190, "Stories" in "Preparing the lessons").
- For Section 2: Find six participants who are willing to act out the skit.
- For Section 4: If needed, prepare slips of paper or index cards with Bible verses or download the Bible verses PDF.
- For Closing: Determine if you will use the Container exercise or Tree exercise (last page of lesson).

In this lesson we will:

- Discuss the need to care for ourselves, especially when helping traumatized people.
- Identify difficulties we face in caring for others.
- Assess how well we are caring for ourselves.
- Illustrate the need for self-care from the Bible.
- Set goals for self-care.

14

Section 1: Story	10 min
Section 2: How can we know if a caregiver is overloaded or has secondary trauma?	20 min
Section 3: Why is it difficult to be a caregiver?	20 min
Section 4: How can caregivers take care of themselves?	30 min
Closing	10-25 min
Total time	**1 hour 30-45 minutes**

14. Caring for the caregiver

F | *(1 min) Introduce lesson title and objectives. Direct participants to the corresponding lesson in Healing the Wounds of Trauma.*

Section 1.   10 min

Pastor Jay

F | *(5 min) Large group. Present the story.*

Pastor Jay has been working hard since two of the big factories in the town shut down. Many people lost their jobs and are losing their housing. Crime is increasing. People from his church are coming to him and he has heard one heartbreaking story after another. He thinks that, as a pastor, he should always be ready to listen, to attend to their requests, and to try to help them find work and housing.

One of Pastor Jay's best friends, Manuel, also lost his job. Pastor Jay does all he can to help out, but with no income and no savings, sometimes Manuel's family has had to go to bed without dinner. One night while Manuel and his family were sleeping, two armed men broke in through their bedroom window. They put a gun to Manuel's head and warned the family members that if they moved, they would kill them. The family stayed completely still while they watched the men take all their food and valuables. Since then, they all sleep in one room at night. Manuel often wakes up afraid, and then realizes that it was only a dream. Manuel came to Pastor Jay and told him about the attack in great detail.

Since Manuel's visit, Pastor Jay cannot stop thinking about what his friend told him. He is not sleeping well. He wakes at the slightest sound. He has lost his energy and gets up very tired. Last week, he woke up three times with terrifying nightmares of robbers breaking into his home and holding him up at gunpoint. He feels like a failure as a pastor and doesn't like preaching anymore. He's thinking of resigning.

His wife is concerned because he rarely speaks to her. Yesterday, he was distracted by his thoughts as he headed to church and had an accident. He broke his leg and his car was totally wrecked.

DISCUSSION

F | *(5 min) Large group.*

1. Why do you think Pastor Jay is having all these problems?
2. Have you ever felt like Pastor Jay? Explain.

F | *If the participants are using books, encourage them to keep them closed as much as possible for the rest of the lesson.*

How can we know if we are overloaded or have secondary trauma?

> F | *(6 min) Mention section title. Have six participants act out the Naomi skit (footnote) as you read it. Then discuss how Naomi feels. Afterward, ask, "What kinds of roles could cause people to be overloaded? What caregiving roles do you have?"*
>
> *(1 min) Ask, "What do we mean by being overloaded?" Get feedback, then add content below ("Overloaded") that was not mentioned.*

Overloaded: We are overloaded when we try to do too many things and have too much responsibility, without getting enough rest.

> F | *(1 min) Ask, "What is secondary trauma?" Get feedback, then add content below ("Secondary trauma") that was not mentioned.*

Secondary trauma: When we listen to people's stories of trauma and grief, we may absorb some of their pain and experience some of the same symptoms they are experiencing (reliving, avoiding, or being on alert all the time). This is referred to as "secondary trauma." It is not the same as being overloaded, but a person could be both overloaded and experiencing secondary trauma.

DISCUSSION

> F | *(5 min) Large group. After the discussion, add content below the questions that was not mentioned.*

Do you know people who have become so overloaded helping others that they became very discouraged or sick? What do they say? How do they behave?

Taking care of other people can wear us out. We can get so busy caring for others that we do not take time to care for ourselves. We may be overloaded if we are:
- Feeling angry or sad all the time.
- Feeling tired and irritable.
- Not sleeping well.
- Having problems with relationships.
- Becoming ill or having many accidents.
- Resenting those who need our help.
- Not interested in work anymore.
- Questioning the truth of our faith.

Naomi skit

Naomi is an overloaded mother who has too many responsibilities. Her husband needs clean clothes, her children need their lunches made, her elderly in-laws are complaining, and her neighbor comes over in tears and wants to talk about her brother's suicide. Naomi gets a phone call from the church, asking her to arrange meals for a woman who has just had a baby.

14

- Questioning God's goodness and power.
- Beginning to believe the lies of Satan about who we are and what we do.

If we have some of these symptoms for a long time, we need to make changes in our life. Our own heart wounds that have not healed may get in the way of our attempts to help others. And if we allow ourselves to become exhausted, we will not be able to carry on with the work God has given us.

DISCUSSION IN PAIRS

F | *(5 min) Pairs.*

Have you ever felt overloaded or experienced secondary trauma? Describe how you felt.

F | *(2 min) Get a little feedback, but do not pressure anyone to share who does not want to.*

Fig. 14.1: An overloaded pastor

Section 3.

20 min

Why is it difficult to be a caregiver?

DISCUSSION

F | *(5 min) Small group.*

What are some things that make it difficult to care for others?

F | *(10 min) Large group. Get feedback. Add content below that was not mentioned.*

Caregivers may face some of the following difficulties.

A. Caregivers may be caring for too many people.

Caregivers may think they are indispensable to God's work and have to personally care for everyone. In addition, the people they care for may think that the caregiver has to do everything. This can be especially true for pastors or priests. Church members may want to talk only to the pastor/priest and no one else.

B. Caregivers may be the object of people's anger.

People who have experienced trauma may feel angry. They may lash out without reason at the people around them. They may show anger toward caregivers who are trying to help. Remembering this can help caregivers not to take the anger personally.

C. Caregivers may be manipulated by people.

Some people who come with problems are not really seeking solutions. Some want to blame others and are not interested in making any changes themselves. Others may just want attention. These people can take up a lot of time. Caregivers need to discern those who really want help from those who are merely seeking attention.

D. Caregivers may find out certain things in confidence that they must tell others.

When people share their problems with a caregiver, what they say should be held in confidence. Some things, however, cannot be kept secret. These may include plans that would hurt someone, abuse of a child, or plans of suicide. Find out the things that must legally be reported in your area. Tell the people ahead of time that these things must be reported to the authorities.

14

E. Caregivers may find that they enjoy being at the center of everything.

Caregivers may like the feeling of being important and needed by so many people. Or sometimes helping others may be a way of avoiding looking at their own problems. These are not good reasons for helping others. Caregivers need to look at their own motives for helping others to be sure they are giving care for good reasons.

F. Caregivers may neglect taking care of themselves.

Caregivers may think they should be strong enough to bear heavy burdens without complaining or becoming angry. But if they don't acknowledge when they feel angry, sad, or afraid, they run the risk of spiritual and emotional exhaustion. And if they neglect taking care of their bodies by working nonstop, not eating well, not sleeping enough, or not getting exercise, they will run out of energy and may even collapse.

G. Caregivers may neglect their own family.

Caring for people takes time. Caregivers can easily spend so much time with others that their own family is neglected. Spouses may become depressed or angry. Children may feel angry that their parent has time for everyone else but no time for them. The parent may not be at home enough to care for and instruct them. Eventually, caregivers who neglect their families will face serious problems.

DISCUSSION

F | *(5 min) Small groups or pairs.*

What is the most difficult thing for you about being a caregiver?

Section 4.   30 min

How can caregivers take care of themselves?

DISCUSSION

F | *(3 min) Large group. Hold up a cell phone and charger, then ask the discussion questions. (Other options are using a blunt pencil or knife and a sharpener, or a water container with a water tap that runs dry. Adjust the questions as needed.) Then present the content below the questions.*

1. What will happen to this phone if it is never charged?
2. Is the time it takes to recharge it wasted or well-used?

We are God's instruments for good in the world. If instruments are not taken care of, they will break, run down, and lose their usefulness. Just as we must take time to recharge a cell phone or sharpen a knife or a pencil, so we must stop and care for ourselves. Then we will be able to take care of others. When we listen to many people, the burden of all their pain can wear us down. We have to be careful not to be crushed by it.

DISCUSSION

F | *(5 min) Small group. Divide the verses among the groups.*

What do the following verses say about caring for ourselves?

1 Kings 19:3–8	Luke 5:15–16	Mark 1:35–39
Galatians 6:2	Exodus 18:13–23	Mark 6:31

F | *(17 min) Large group. Get feedback. Add content below that was not mentioned.*

A. Let God care for you.

The Bible gives examples of God's servants who were so tired that they could not continue their work. God gave them special care at that time. God took care of Elijah when he was tired and discouraged (1 Kings 19:3–8). Jesus withdrew from the demands of the crowds and prayed (Luke 5:15–16). God has promised to comfort us, help us, and be strong for us when we are overwhelmed. He understands that we are weak. Even Jesus got tired and sad and felt troubled (John 4:6; Mark 4:34–40; Matthew 26:36–46). Take time in prayer to know God's love and care for you.

B. Recognize that even Jesus, our prime example, did not help everyone.

When we see many needs, we may feel responsible to respond to all of them. Jesus did not heal every sick or hurting person in each town he visited. He regularly spent time alone with God, to let his Father guide him in everything, including when it was time to move from one village to the next (Mark 1:35–39).

C. Share your burdens with others.

Have regular times for sharing and prayer with a small group or another person. Share with other caregivers or mature Christians. In the same way that people who have experienced trauma need to talk it out, caregivers need to share their burdens with others (Galatians 6:2).

D. Share the workload with others.

When Moses was overwhelmed with work, he took his father-in-law's advice and selected people with whom he could share the work (Exodus 18:13–23). Sharing the workload means, first of all, giving up some of the control of your ministry. Others can begin to take some of the load from your shoulders. Even though they may do things differently than you do, they will learn how to serve and you will no longer be the only one people look to for help.

Pastors and priests can identify others in the church who are mature and who are gifted in helping others. It is good to have a balanced team of people: men and women, from different ages and ethnic groups (Romans 12:4–8). Train them to help others, and then let the people know that they can go to them for help when they have problems. Help church members understand that people besides the pastor or priest can help them. God intended for all Christians to minister to one another (Galatians 6:2; James 5:16). You will find satisfaction in training others well and seeing them succeed. Help church members understand that you will be able to work better if you can take time to "recharge."

E. Take time away from the situation.

Find opportunities to rest and get away from the difficulties and pain, even if only for a short time. Jesus and his disciples did (Mark 6:31). Sometimes it takes several days—even weeks—of rest to begin to release the burden. Developing a regular practice of setting aside work and quieting your soul makes it less likely that you will become overwhelmed by all you have to do.

Pastors need to reserve time for their spouse and children, since they are part of their ministry, not a barrier to it. A family retreat or holiday might be appropriate.

F. Take care of your body.

> F | *(5 min) Ask, "What are ways you can take care of your body?" Get feedback. Add content below that was not mentioned.*

- Get exercise daily. Exercise releases stress.
- Get enough sleep. Adults need seven to eight hours per night.
- Eat good, nourishing food. If money for food is limited, learn about healthy but less expensive options. Don't become so busy with work that you forget to eat. You need good food to be strong physically.

Closing

F | *(5–10 min) Read the questions, then give participants time to reflect.*

Take time in silence, reflecting on the following questions:

1. Think about your workload. How can you care for yourself and your family as you care for others?
2. What do you think God wants you to change to care better for yourself?
3. What is one specific thing you can do in the next week to better care for yourself?

F | *Encourage participants to share their "one thing" with their spouse, coworker, or a close friend in the next twenty-four hours. **Optional:** (5 min) In pairs, have participants share about what they discovered in their individual time, then pray for each other.*
   (5–10 min) Lead participants through one of the exercises below. Read the text slowly enough to allow people to imagine each part.

CONTAINER EXERCISE

Sometimes we can be overwhelmed by what we have experienced but we are not in a situation where we can express how we feel. This exercise can be helpful.

If you feel comfortable doing so, close your eyes, or just look down at the floor so you are not distracted. Imagine a big container. It could be a big box or a shipping container. Imagine a way to lock the container, like a key or a padlock.

Now imagine putting all the things that are disturbing you right now into the container: big things, small things—everything that is disturbing you. You may need to think of a symbol to represent some of these things, for example an air ticket to represent a traumatic plane flight. When they are all inside the container, close it. Now lock the container and put the key somewhere safe. Do not throw it away. When you are ready, open your eyes and look up.

Later, find a time when you can get quiet. Take the key, open the container, and take out the things you have put inside one by one. You may want to do this with someone who can help you talk about these things. You may need a number of separate sessions to take out these things one by one. Do not leave them in the container forever!

TREE EXERCISE

This is an exercise for increasing resiliency. Doing this exercise when you are not under stress will help you be able to relax in times of stress.

Sit quietly and, if you feel comfortable, close your eyes. Reflect on this passage from Psalm 1.

> *Happy are those who reject the advice of evil people,*
> *who do not follow the example of sinners*
> *or join those who have no use for God.*
> *Instead, they find joy in obeying the Law of the Lord,*
> *and they study it day and night.*

They are like trees that grow beside a stream,
that bear fruit at the right time,
and whose leaves do not dry up.
They succeed in everything they do. (Psalm 1:1–3)

Imagine that you are a tree.

- What kind of tree would you be? See yourself as that kind of tree.
- In your imagination, look around. Is your tree by itself?
- What's the landscape around you?

Now look at the trunk of the tree.

- Notice it going down into the earth and up into the branches. Follow the branches way out into the leaves. (If it's a fruit tree: See the fruit hanging from the branches).

Now follow the trunk down to the roots.

- Look at the roots—is it a long single root or many roots going out? Notice how the roots are anchored into the ground.
- Now watch how the root system is bringing water and nutrients to the roots and how those nutrients travel up the tree to the branches.

Notice the weather.

- Imagine the sun shining on the leaves, making oxygen. Imagine the tree just being there with just the right temperature and light.
- Now the tree needs a bit of water. Imagine a gentle rain slowly coming down over the leaves and going towards the roots. See the water going down, down into the roots. See the moisture being taken up into the tree.
- Now stop the rain and imagine the sun coming out again to dry the leaves.

Now imagine the tree with some live creatures—perhaps birds, or squirrels or insects going up and down. Watch all the activity.

Now there's a storm.

- Black clouds are beginning to form in the distance. The storm won't harm or destroy the tree, but the storm *will* come.
- The wind is picking up and the clouds are coming. The branches are shaking. The trunk is moving back and forth. Some of the leaves are falling and some of the fruit is falling.
- Now focus on how the roots are holding firm and allowing the tree to move back and forth in the wind. Let the storm go on a bit. Feel the tree moving back and forth with its roots firmly planted in the ground.
- Now the storm is slowing gradually until everything is still again.
- How is the tree feeling after the storm?
- Now the sun is returning. The insects and birds are coming back out again. Things are drying. Imagine the tree coming back to normal.

When the tree is still again, the sun is shining, the insects and the birds are back out again, gradually take some deep breaths and open your eyes.

14

15. How can we live as Christians in the midst of conflict?

This lesson can arouse a lot of emotions, depending on the context and who is in the group. Get advice from local people as you prepare to facilitate.

Before you begin:

- For Section 1: Decide whether you will use the Acts 6 skit or the story. If you use the skit, find someone who is willing to be Peter and give them Peter's lines. If you use the story, decide how you will present it (see page 190, "Stories" in "Preparing the lessons"). If you decide to use both the skit and the story, adjust your total time.
- For Section 2: Choose which exercise you will do (conflict tree exercise or prejudices exercise) and prepare the large piece(s) of paper for each table group. If you decide to use both exercises, adjust your total time.
- For Sections 2 and 3: If needed, prepare slips of paper or index cards with Bible verses or download the Bible verses PDF.
- For the Closing: If you will be doing the peace tree exercise, get a large piece of paper for each group.

In this lesson we will:

- Discuss the fact that conflict is a part of life, even in the church.
- Identify the roots of conflict, especially prejudice.
- Discuss how to live as a Christian with integrity in the midst of conflict.
- Explore how to serve as a bridge between sides of a conflict to bring reconciliation.

Section 1: Story	15 min
Section 2: What are some causes of conflict between groups?	45–50 min
Section 3: How can we live as Christians in the midst of conflict?	20 min
Section 4: How can we help bring reconciliation?	15 min
Closing	10–30 min
Total time	**1 hour 45 minutes – 2 hours 10 minutes**

15. How can we live as Christians in the midst of conflict?

F *(1 min) Introduce lesson title and objectives. Direct participants to the corresponding lesson in Healing the Wounds of Trauma. Present the content below.*

Trauma can be a cause of conflict and a result of conflict. This lesson is intended to help people address conflict in a way that reduces the likelihood of future trauma. This can contribute to reconciliation, but political leaders will eventually need to be involved to solve national-level conflicts.

Since the church is multiethnic and involves people from all social classes, hidden tensions can often surface in veiled ways even if there is no overt conflict.

Section 1.

15 min

Two stories of conflict

A. Church conflict

F *(10 min) Have the group act out this skit spontaneously, using the prompts in italics to direct the skit. Do not tell the participants it is a Bible passage beforehand except one person: the person who plays the role of Peter. Have him read Acts 6:1–7 beforehand and be ready to say, "Stop! It's not right for us to stop studying and preaching God's word in order to distribute food. So, choose some wise men to put in charge of this problem."*

SKIT

In a large church in the capital city, trouble was brewing. This church was known for taking care of the widows in the congregation. At this time there were two groups of widows, and both groups were good Christians.

The first group of widows had always lived in the homeland. *(Choose a group of people and send them to one side to look like sad widows.)* Every day, the church sent some workers to give these widows food and the other things they needed. *(Choose a group of people to carry food and clothes to the widows. The widows should look happy.)*

The second group of widows was made up of women who were displaced by war and had lived in another country so long that they no longer spoke their own language. *(Choose a group of people to be the second group of widows. Put them at a distance from the first group. They should act like sad widows as well.)* The church sent them food as well. *(Have another group of people start taking food and clothes to them).*

One day the widows who used to live abroad started complaining that they were getting less food than the widows who had always lived there. *(Have the second group of widows start yelling and complaining.)* Soon many in the church got involved in the argument. *(Have the servers of food start arguing, some on the side of one group of widows, some on the other—by now all of them should be shouting and arguing.)*

(Now have "Peter" walk in and say:) "Stop! It's not right for us to stop studying and preaching God's word in order to distribute food. So, choose some wise men to put in charge of this problem."

(Say:) The church members thought this was good and chose some people from each side. *(Have them do this.)*

> F | *If they have not realized it by now, tell them that this is the story in Acts 6. Then read this summary of Acts 6.*

At the time when the church was just beginning, many Jews had been displaced, and were living in foreign countries. They lived there so long that they took on the customs and language of their adopted country. They feared God and continued to worship him and made trips back to Jerusalem as often as possible. They believed it was good to be buried in the homeland, so older couples moved back to Israel if they could. Often the husband died first, leaving his widow in need of someone to provide for her.

Meanwhile, the Jews who stayed in Israel through the years continued to follow their customs and speak their own language. They felt that because they had never left their land or traditions, they were better in God's eyes. Even though they were poorer, they looked down on the foreign Jews.

One of the traditions of the early church was to care for widows, as taught in the Bible. Most of the earliest Christians were Jews. They took care of the foreign Jewish widows just like they took care of their own. But there were so many foreign Jewish widows that the homeland Jews had a hard time caring for them.

It wasn't long before tensions formed between the homeland Jews and the foreign Jews. The foreign Jews complained that their widows were not being given their share when food was handed out each day. So the apostles called a meeting to address the problem openly. They realized that these ethnic tensions could destroy the church. They said, "It's not right for us to give up God's word in order to distribute food. So, brothers and sisters, choose seven men who are respected, wise, and full of the Holy Spirit. We will put them in charge of this problem."

The church chose seven men. At least one of these men was from the group of foreign Jews. They dealt with the problem, and the church continued to grow. The unity between the foreign Jews and those who stayed in the homeland was a strong testimony to those outside the church. (Summary of Acts 6)

DISCUSSION

> F | *(5 min) Large group.*

1. What might the foreign Jewish women have been thinking and feeling?
2. What might the homeland Jewish women have been thinking and feeling?
3. What can we learn from this passage about resolving conflict?

> F | *If the participants are using books, encourage them to keep them closed as much as possible for the rest of the lesson.*

B. Nate and Paul

F | (5 min) Large group. Present the story.

Nate was married, had three children, and originally came from Kizi. He grew up in a neighborhood made up mainly of people from Kizi. A few years later, a huge influx of immigrants from Mora started coming in. Hostility began to build as the Kizis saw Mora families taking over "their" houses, jobs, schools, and even their place as the largest minority population in the city. Every day Nate grumbled about the situation as he walked through his old neighborhood on his way to work.

Paul had emigrated from Mora with his wife and four children. Even though it was difficult to adjust to this new country, he found it to be a land of opportunity. He couldn't understand how the Kizis could be so lazy. He stayed as far away from them as he could because he thought they were thieves and no good.

One day, Nate and Paul were both nominated as representatives for a special parent committee at the school. Hesitantly, they both accepted, and the group began to meet every week. At the meetings, the Kizis and the Moras avoided each other. But as the meetings went on, Nate and Paul got interested in the issues the school was facing and began talking together.

Nate couldn't believe how industrious Paul was, working more than sixty hours a week at two jobs on opposite sides of the city! Paul was surprised to hear Nate talk about how much he wanted to keep the kids in school and off the streets so they could have good lives. Nate shared about his dream of children going to college and getting good jobs so they could provide for their families. He told Paul about the basketball team he had organized to get to know the young boys. Paul began to appreciate Nate's warmth and concern for the kids. Maybe, he thought, Nate wasn't a lazy thief.

As they went on talking week after week, they discovered they were both Christians. They had never really imagined that someone from the other group could be a real Christian!

Finally one night, Nate said to Paul, "You know, I wanted to run all Moras out of the neighborhood, but now I see how we could work together to make this a great place!"

Paul said, "You know, I always thought your people were lazy, but I don't feel that way anymore."

Nate said, "Do you ever play basketball?"

"No, but my sons would really like to learn," said Paul.

Nate said, "Why don't you all come over to my house? How about this Saturday?"

DISCUSSION

F | (5 min) Small groups or pairs. Have each group select someone to take notes and speak for the group. (If possible, have the group select a different person for each small group discussion going forward.)

1. Why did Nate and Paul find it hard to accept that the other one was a real Christian?
2. How might the friendship between Nate and Paul affect their families and communities?

F | (5 min) Large group. Get feedback. If the participants are using books, encourage them to keep them closed as much as possible for the rest of the lesson.

What are some causes of conflict between groups?

F | *(5 min) Ask, "What comes into your mind when you hear the word 'conflict'?" Give one minute for individual reflection, then get answers from several people.*

DISCUSSION

F | *(5 min) Large group or small group. Ask this question to identify the type of conflict(s) you will focus on later in the lesson.*

1. What kinds of conflict affect your community?

F | *If people have trouble answering the question, ask one of the following questions:*
   - *What different groups in our community or country have disagreements or tensions?*
   - *Do people in one group believe that their difficulties were caused by another group?*
   - *Does it seem that certain groups enjoy privileges while others are victims of discrimination?*
   - *Do both sides of the conflict perceive that they were the victims in history?*

DISCUSSION

F | *(8 min) Small group. Divide the topics and verses among the groups or pairs.*

2. What do the verses and topics below reveal about the causes of conflicts between groups?
   - Desire for resources. James 4:1–3
   - Ineffective or unjust governments. Proverbs 29:4
   - People who stir up conflict. 2 Samuel 20:1–2
   - A history of prejudice. Acts 10:34–35, 11:1–3
3. Can you think of examples in your country/region where this has happened?

F | *(12 min) Large group. Get feedback, then add content below that was not mentioned.*

A. Desire for resources

We may desire to have something so strongly that we are willing to fight for it. This can lead to conflict and sometimes violence (James 4:1–3). We may fight over land or water or political power, for example. We may be greedy and want more than our share of resources, or fearful because resources are running short, or fearful that others will take what we have from us.

B. Ineffective or unjust governments

God has put governments in place to see that people receive justice (Romans 13:1–4; 1 Timothy 2:1–2). If governments neglect justice (Proverbs 29:4) and there is widespread suffering and insecurity, people become angry and rebel, or they flee to other regions where they may come into conflict with people there. In times of political instability, old conflicts between groups resurface because there is no one to stop them.

C. People who stir up conflict

Some individuals stir up conflict to gain power for themselves (2 Samuel 20:1–2). The newspapers, social media, and radio can also fan the flames of blame, fear, and hatred. Once violence starts, it is difficult to stop.

D. A history of prejudice

Children often learn prejudice and distrust of other groups from their parents and other family or community members. When we hear stories about people from another group doing bad things, it is easy to believe that all the people from that group are like that. Memory of a bad experience, or an event that happened in the previous generation, may cause a person to distrust all the people in the other group, or desire to get revenge. Prejudices keep people from ever finding out what the other group is really like (Acts 10:34–35, 11:1–3). Many people are not aware of the prejudices they have.

In times of conflict, problems are often blamed on the other group. To be able to treat others cruelly, we learn to think of them as less than human. Meanwhile, people will often see their own group as superior and entitled to privileges. For example, a group may feel entitled to special respect and service from those who were their slaves earlier in history.

SMALL GROUP ACTIVITY

F | *(15–20 min) Do one of the options. If short on time, do the exercise as a large group activity.*

Option 1: Conflict tree exercise

F | *(5–10 min) Small groups. Give a large piece of paper to each small group, then present the exercise content.*

Draw a tree on a large piece of paper, with the roots showing. This tree represents a community divided by conflict. Identify a conflict you would like to discuss. Write it on the trunk of the tree. Discuss the following question:

1. What are the fruits (the outcomes) of this conflict?

Draw and label the fruits on the tree. Then discuss:

2. What are the roots (the causes) of this conflict?

As the roots are identified, write them on the roots of the tree.

In order to solve conflict, a group needs to address the roots, not the fruit. This is usually a long-term task beyond the ability of the group to resolve, but this exercise can help them recognize the underlying issues and address them at their level of influence.

F | *(10 min) Post the tree drawings on the wall and have each group briefly explain their tree. In the large group discuss, "What did you learn from this exercise, and what was difficult?"*

***Time-saver:** Let people look at the drawings during breaks instead of doing oral presentations.*

Fig. 15.1: Example of a conflict tree

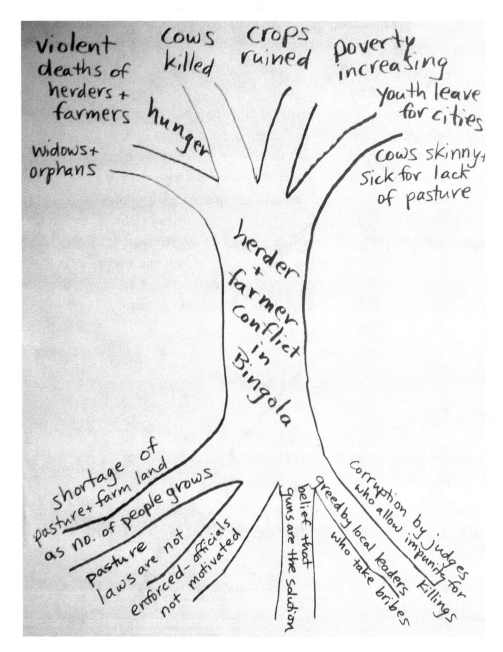

Option 2: Prejudices discussion

F | *(10 min) Small groups or pairs.*

1. What are some prejudices you may have inherited about another group? Can you think of any examples that would show these ideas are not true?
2. How do others describe your group? What examples might they have for this description?

F | *(10 min) Large group. Get feedback.*

Section 3.

How can we live as Christians in the midst of conflict?

F | *(1 min) Mention the section title. Present the content below.*

God calls Christians to be salt and light, bringing the good news of Jesus Christ into evil and dark situations (Matthew 5:13–16; Philippians 2:14–16). The Bible encourages Christians not to be overcome by evil but to overcome evil with good (Romans 12:21).

Conflict between Christians is a special cause of concern, as it affects the testimony of Christ in the world. Jesus said: "I pray that they may all be one. Father! May they be in us, just as you are in me and I am in you. May they be one, so that the world will believe that you sent me" (John 17:21). Christians are to have their minds transformed by Christ. This means that they should react differently from non-Christians (Romans 12:1–2). This is the path of blessing, but it is not an easy path and we must choose to follow it.

DISCUSSION

F | *(5 min) Small group. Read the discussion question out loud. Distribute the topics and verses among small groups or pairs, to read their verse and answer the question. If desired, substitute 2 Corinthians 12:9–10 for 2 Timothy 3:16–17 in "Receive strength from God" (see D).*

What do we learn from these topics and verses about living with conflict?
- Communicate honestly and lovingly with others. Ephesians 4:25–27; Colossians 3:12–14
- Put loyalty to Christ before loyalty to any group. 1 Peter 1:3–6; 2 Corinthians 5:16–18
- Do not take revenge but show love and work for justice. Romans 12:19–21; Psalm 82:3
- Receive strength from God and trust that God will achieve his purposes. 2 Timothy 3:16–17; Matthew 10:28–31

F | *(14 min) Large group. Get feedback, then add content below that was not mentioned.*

A. Communicate honestly and lovingly with others
- Speak honestly rather than ignoring or covering up our feelings (Ephesians 4:25).
- Address issues before they develop into a conflict (Ephesians 4:26–27).
- Model to others the love and forgiveness God has given you (Colossians 3:12–14).
- Don't gossip. Discuss problems only with those who are part of the problem and can be part of the solution (Matthew 18:15–17).
- Talk about how we felt and how the other person's behavior affects us ("I felt hurt …") instead of accusing or blaming the other person.
- Use good listening skills to try to understand the other person ("Help me understand …" "Tell me more …")
- Explore ways to make things right.

B. Put loyalty to Christ before loyalty to any group

- Realize that even if everything else is taken from us—our family members, our homes, our possessions, our work, our own lives—Christ can never be taken from us (1 Peter 1:3–6).
- Give up our cultural prejudices, with God's help. Old ways of judging others must go (2 Corinthians 5:16–18).
- Realize that God has no favorites; all people are treated equally by him (Acts 10:34; Romans 2:9–11).
- Cherish our new identity as part of God's holy nation along with all believers from around the world (1 Peter 2:9; Revelation 5:9–10).

C. Do not take revenge but show love and work for justice

- Do not take revenge for the wrongs done to us or our families but show love and allow God to punish others (Romans 12:19–21; Matthew 5:38–42). Revenge does not bring peace to our hearts or bring back what was lost. It only perpetuates violence.
- Respect human life as created in God's image (Genesis 1:27). Do not harm or mistreat others.
- Work for justice and uphold the rights of the poor and oppressed (Psalm 82:3). Speak up for those who cannot speak for themselves (Proverbs 31:8).
- Whenever possible, use nonviolent means to defend those who are in danger of being mistreated. The most powerful thing Jesus did was to make himself completely vulnerable to his enemies while he was on the cross (1 Peter 2:21–23). People like Gandhi in India and Martin Luther King Jr. in the United States have challenged governments by standing against evil without using violence. These movements have resulted in correcting widespread injustice more effectively than a violent reaction could have, and those involved were not guilty of shedding blood.

D. Receive strength from God and trust that God will achieve his purposes

- Let Scripture transform us (2 Timothy 3:16–17; Romans 12:1–2).
- Spend time apart with God, and include the practice of lament, so God can restore our souls (Mark 6:31, 45–46).
- Ask the Holy Spirit for power, especially when we are weak (2 Corinthians 12:9–10; Acts 1:8).
- Meet with other Christians to share our pain and pray for one another (Hebrews 10:25; James 5:16).
- Trust that God sees what happens to us (Matthew 10:28–31).
- Know that God works for our good even in evil situations (Romans 8:28). Both Joseph and Jesus suffered, but God used their suffering for good (Genesis 45:5–7; Acts 3:13–15). God is at work, in spite of people's evil intentions.
- Remember that our lives are not our own. God knows the date of our death before we're even born (Psalm 139:15–16). If we have been spared while others have died, it is because God still has a purpose for our lives (Esther 4:13–14; 2 Thessalonians 1:11–12).

Section 4.

How can we help bring reconciliation?

DISCUSSION

F | *(15 min) Large group. After the discussion, add content from A–D that was not mentioned.*

How can we help bring reconciliation?

Fig. 15.2: Becoming a bridge

A. We can become a bridge between the groups in conflict

- We may need to sacrifice our need to belong to a group in order to become a bridge between the two groups in conflict. For example, we should share food and resources with those in need, no matter which side they are on.
- We need to love our enemies (Matthew 5:43–48) and treat them as brothers. This may put our lives at risk. Our enemies may want to harm us, and members of our own group may see us as traitors who should be punished.
- We can remember we are aliens in this world, particularly if we do not know any other peacemakers in the situation (Hebrews 11:13–16). We may be alone with God as our only friend (Matthew 5:9).
- We can spend time listening to both groups, to try to understand the pain that each side of the conflict has experienced from their perspective. Then we can help each side understand the pain of the other, give up prejudice, and view the other as human (Romans 12:17–21). If we hear too much from one side, we may begin to see only their point of view.
- In places where peacemakers from both sides of the conflict work together, progress is possible by God's grace (James 3:17–18).

B. We can help people bring their pain to Christ for healing

- Where there is conflict, nearly everyone has wounds of the heart. These should be brought to Christ so he can heal the pain.
- Where people have sinned against others, they must repent and ask for forgiveness from God and from those they have hurt.
- When Christ has broken down barriers between us, we need to celebrate and praise him together (Ephesians 2:14). He is Lord. He sets us free from the lies and traps of the enemy.

C. We can repent of the sins of our group

- The worst things that happen in the world are caused not by individuals, but by groups: ethnic groups, governments, religious groups.
- Even if we were not involved personally in doing wrong, we can repent before God on behalf of our group, both for things done currently and things done by previous generations (Leviticus 26:40; Daniel 9:4–9; Nehemiah 9:1–37; Ezra 9:5–15).
- We can ask forgiveness of those who have been hurt by our group.
- When one group repents and asks forgiveness, it can lead to the other group repenting as well, and reconciliation follows.

D. Groups should discuss their problems openly and find solutions

- If people's heart wounds have begun to heal, they may be ready to address the deeper problems that started the conflict.
- All people who are affected need to be well represented in the discussion.
- Let each side express their perspective while the other side listens, and then have the other side summarize what they have heard.
- People need to work together, compromise, and find ways to live together that are seen as generally acceptable to all (Acts 6:1–7).

Closing   10-30 min

F | *Choose one of the closing exercises. Give participants time to reflect on the "one thing" question at the end.*

Option 1: Peace tree exercise

F | *(10–30 min) Small group. Give a large piece of paper to each small group, then present the exercise content. If the participants will have the opportunity to identify and undertake concrete actions in their communities, more time should be allowed for this section to discuss action plans after doing the tree.*

Draw a tree on a large piece of paper, with roots showing. Write "Peace" on the tree's trunk. This tree represents the positive things that could help your community resolve their conflicts. Discuss the following question:

1. What could be the roots (the causes) of this peace and reconciliation?

As the roots are identified, write them on the roots of the tree. Then discuss:

2. What could be the fruits (the outcomes) of this peace and reconciliation?

Draw and label the fruits on the tree. Look at the peace tree pictures together. Form a circle to pray for God's strength to take these actions to bring peace.

Option 2: Bridge exercise

F │ *(15 min) Mark off an imaginary river in the middle of the room. Present the exercise content, as you divide the participants into two groups and place each group on opposite sides of the river. Decide as a group what the conflict is between the two sides.*

A river flows through the middle of this room. One group is camped on each side of the river. They are in conflict. In small groups, find something that symbolizes what you could do to make a bridge between the two groups. Then explain your symbol as you lay it over the river.

F │ *Give the groups time to find their symbol and explain it.*

Option 3: Self-reflection exercise

F │ *(10 min) Pairs.*

In pairs, share about a time you were involved in a conflict.
*   How did you feel?
*   What was the hardest part?
*   What helped you find healing?
Pray for each other.

What is one thing you want to remember from this lesson?

16. Preparing for trouble

Before you begin:

- For Section 1: Decide how you will present the story (see page 190, "Stories" in "Preparing the lessons").
- For Section 4: Be sure you know how to program emergency contact numbers into a cell phone so you can demonstrate for participants.
- For Section 5: If needed, prepare slips of paper or index cards with Bible verses or download the Bible verses PDF.

In this lesson we will:

- Show from the Bible that it is wise to prepare for trouble.
- Discuss how individuals and families can prepare for trouble.
- Discuss how to help the community prepare physically and spiritually for trouble.
- Discuss how the community can organize communication channels in case of crisis.

Section 1: Story	10 min
Section 2: Why should we prepare for the future?	5 min
Section 3: How can we prepare practically?	25 min
Section 4: How can we be ready to communicate when trouble comes?	20 min
Section 5: How can we prepare spiritually for difficult situations?	40 min
Closing	5 min
Total time	**1 hour 45 minutes**

16. Preparing for trouble

F | *(1 min) Introduce lesson title and objectives. Direct participants to the corresponding lesson in Healing the Wounds of Trauma.*

Section 1.   **10 min**

Hurricane season soon

F | *(5 min) Large group. Present the story.*

"Hurricane season soon…. How do we prepare for it?" The new priest, Doug, was sitting with his church committee for the first time after his arrival in the coastal town.

"Prepare? What does it have to do with us as a church?" asked the committee chair, Al, rather crossly. "That's the government's job."

"Well," said Doug, "in my last church we were able to help the local community after a major hurricane by opening the church to people who had lost their homes, and by supplying blankets and food."

"Hmmm. Well, let's get on with the important church business on this agenda," said Al, as he passed around some lists.

Two months later the news was full of the devastation being caused in the south by Hurricane Tom. The weather forecasters warned that this storm was likely to hit the mainland right near Doug's town. Some of Doug's church members immediately boarded up their houses and left town to stay with friends and relations.

Al and his wife Sue were well past retirement age and lived in a prefabricated home near the ocean. Some other church members lived in a mobile home complex. Many of them decided to stay, even though their homes were not sturdy. Some had nowhere to go, but others stayed just because they had survived other hurricanes in the past.

Doug got in contact with people in the town government. They were urging everyone near the coast to leave. Doug became concerned about the vulnerable people in his congregation and started preparing the church's fellowship hall to receive people. He thought about what would happen when the power went out and was able to get battery-powered and hand-cranked lights, as well as propane stoves, camp cots, blankets, canned food, and bottled water to store in the church.

The hurricane struck. It was a terrifying experience for everyone still in the town. The wind knocked down trees, the sea swamped houses people thought were well inland from the shore, and there was flooding along many streets. As soon as the storm eased a little, Doug started checking on his parishioners, particularly the older ones and those in mobile homes. With the help of the government disaster team, he reached the area where Al lived and found him standing in the rain outside his destroyed house, trying to comfort his distraught wife. Doug quickly got them into his car, took them to the church, and helped make them comfortable in the fellowship hall.

Soon they were joined by others, mainly elderly people from the mobile home complex. There were also some mothers with small children who had lost power in their homes and had no way of preparing meals. By the first evening after the storm, the fellowship hall was full of stunned people who had at least found shelter for the moment. Doug spent some time phoning other churches in the town and arranging for them to take in more people in need.

It took some months before everyone was back in their homes and a new routine was established. One year later, almost on the anniversary of his first meeting with the parish committee, they were meeting again. Doug started by saying, "Hurricane season soon…. How can we prepare for it?" He got a different reaction this time!

DISCUSSION

F   *(5 min) Large group.*

1. Why did the church not prepare in advance for the hurricane?
2. How did Doug prepare for the hurricane?
3. What troubles might you need to prepare for in your area?

F   *If the participants are using books, encourage them to keep them closed as much as possible for the rest of the lesson.*

Section 2.   5 min

Why should we prepare for the future?

DISCUSSION

F   *(5 min) Large group. After the discussion, add content below the question that was not mentioned.*

Why should we prepare for troubles?

God's Word says, "Sensible people will see trouble coming and avoid it, but an unthinking person will walk right into it and regret it later" (Proverbs 22:3). God has given us intelligence and common sense and he expects us to use them. Church leaders are responsible before God to lead and look after their congregations (1 Peter 5:1–2; Acts 20:28).

- If the issues have been discussed and plans developed beforehand, it is much easier to respond well when a crisis comes. People in the middle of a crisis often don't have the ability to think clearly.
- Lives can be saved and victims' needs can be better met if plans are developed for the type of troubles that are most common in the area, whether war, riots, terrorist attacks, or natural disasters. For example, if a community lives near a volcano, or in an area subject to flooding, the community can make plans and prepare to help people after a flood or a volcanic eruption.

- If the church works on preparation with the community and local government, this helps to establish good relations between them and to prevent accusations that the church is promoting civil unrest.

There are three areas of preparation that are important: practical preparation, communication, and spiritual preparation.

Section 3. 25 min

How can we prepare practically?

F | *Mention section title.*

DISCUSSION

F | *(7 min) Small group.*

Imagine the following situation: Your family is told that because of an impending crisis (a natural disaster or conflict), you must flee within thirty minutes, taking only what you can carry. What are the most important items to take?

F | *(13 min) Large group. Have each group share a few of the items on their list, until the groups have shared everything on their lists. List these on the board. Then add anything not mentioned from the list below the question. Put less essential items in parentheses. Discuss what a church needs to prepare, in addition to what has already been mentioned. Discuss hiding sensitive or valuable items that are hard to transport.*

Items to take, depending on the location:
- Medicines (prescription and non-prescription, like pain relievers)
- Soap (or hand sanitizer or moist towelettes)
- A first-aid kit
- Food, including salt, for at least three days
- Water
- Matches, in a waterproof container
- A way to boil water and cook
- Identity papers and important financial documents (consider scanning or copying these in advance)
- Written list of important phone numbers and addresses in case cell phones are lost or cannot be charged
- Essential tools (for example, knife, spoon)
- Radio and batteries
- Torch/flashlight

16

- Bible
- Extra clothes and good walking shoes
- Cell phone and charger
- Computer and charger

According to the local situation, other items can be added or left out. If a family really only had thirty minutes to get ready, they would probably leave some important items behind, so prepare a bag of essential items in advance that can be collected quickly if the family needs to leave. Most of the above items could be put into the bag ready to go. Some kinds of food will not spoil.

Church leaders also need to think about church belongings. If possible, they need to take the most important documents with them. In some situations, it could be dangerous for a list of church members or other church documents to fall into the wrong hands.

If you live in an area prone to certain disasters, learn ahead of time which organizations to go to for help.

DISCUSSION

F | *(5 min) Large group. After the discussion, add content below the question that was not mentioned.*

If you had to stay in your home for many days due to a crisis, possibly without electricity or access to clean water, would you need any additional items besides those in the list above?

You may want to consider a water filter or a product that disinfects water, and cheap, safe energy and light sources that do not require electricity. Some locations have emergency preparedness websites that are helpful.

Section 4. 20 min

How can we be ready to communicate when trouble comes?

F | *Mention section title.*

DISCUSSION

F | *(5 min) Small group. Adapt these questions to local situations—e.g. terrorist attacks, different types of disasters, approach of enemy soldiers, and so on.*

Do you or your family have a plan of where to go and how to communicate if a crisis occurs? Does your community/church have such a plan? If so, explain the plans. If not, discuss who should be involved in making these plans.

F | *(15 min) Large group. Get feedback. Add content below that was not mentioned. Consider taking time to help people enter emergency contact numbers into their cell phones.*

A. With our families

Each family should openly discuss what to do if a crisis comes. This discussion should include the children. The family should plan where they will go in case of danger. They should decide on a meeting place if the family gets separated and discuss different routes to get there. They should also decide on a meeting place that is outside of the town, in case the crisis affects the entire town.

Families should discuss how they will try to communicate with each other if they are separated. During a disaster, local phone networks may become overloaded, but text messages may be able to get through. Decide on a relative or friend who lives in a different part of the country, so all family members can call or text to let them know they are safe. Memorize this phone number, as well as family members' phone numbers. Enter emergency contact numbers into your phone.

Even very small children should be taught to say their name and their family name. Children as young as three years old can learn to do this. In one East African war where many families were separated, children who could clearly give this information were reunited with their parents much more rapidly than children who only knew their first name.

Fig. 16.1: A family that prepared for trouble

B. With the churches and the community

Churches and communities should plan how they will communicate with their people during a crisis. Establish a means of communicating with each other, such as alarms, phones, drums/instruments, radio, television, social media, and notes on paper. A good plan includes multiple ways of communicating in case one way no longer works.

Find out in advance the organizations that offer help during various types of crises, and the best way to communicate with them during a crisis.

C. With the outside world

Find out in advance the appropriate way to communicate about a crisis with the outside world. Avoid sharing unverified social media posts. Appropriate information may help bring aid to the area.

Section 5.

How can we prepare spiritually for difficult situations?

F | *Mention section title. Present this content, then mention subpoint A.*

The Bible shows that during our lives we should expect to face trouble, but that God will always be with us in that trouble (John 16:33). God is bigger than the crisis. There are a number of ways we can prepare spiritually for difficult situations.

A. By meditating on the way God has been with his people during troubles in the past

DISCUSSION

F | *(5 min) Large group. Refer to examples below the question if needed.*

What are some examples in the Bible of God being with his people during troubles?

The Bible is filled with stories of how God was with his people during crises. Again and again God opened doors for them, granted them favor in the eyes of authorities, provided deliverance in surprising ways, and gave them courage to face death boldly. Here are a few examples:

- When Joseph was sent to Egypt as a slave, God granted him favor again and again in the eyes of his captors (Genesis 39:1–5, 19–23). God gave Joseph supernatural insight into the famine that was coming and how to respond so that many lives would be saved (Genesis 45:3–8; Acts 7:9–15).
- When a genocide was planned against the Israelites living in Persia, God gave Esther courage and wisdom in interacting with the king. This resulted in deliverance for her people (Esther 4:15–16, 8:3–11).
- The apostle Paul experienced crisis after crisis as he preached the gospel, facing death repeatedly, and being delivered repeatedly (2 Timothy 4:16–18; 2 Corinthians 12:10).
- Stephen was encouraged by seeing Jesus in heaven. This gave him courage as he died, and he was able to forgive his enemies (Acts 7:54–60).
- The writer of the New Testament letter to the Hebrews offers a list of people of faith. Some of them experienced miraculous deliverance, while others did not (Hebrews 11:33–37).

Remembering how God has been with his people in the past can help us trust him when troubles come.

B. By practicing good responses to trouble now

DISCUSSION, IN PAIRS

F | *(5 min) Pairs.*

1. How do you tend to respond to troubles in daily life? Consider feelings, behaviors, thoughts, and patterns of speech.
2. How do you relate to God during trouble?

3. When you face troubles now, how might you handle them more effectively?

F | *(5 min) Large group. Get feedback. Add content below that was not mentioned.*

We can prepare spiritually for a crisis by starting to practice good responses to trouble right now. The way we respond to difficulties today is the same way we will respond to difficulties in the future, either with faith or unbelief. Faith does not mean that we do not experience strong emotions of fear, doubt, confusion, or anger, but that we keep bringing our troubles to God and looking to him for help. We cry out to God and ask others to do so on our behalf. We learn how to cope with those strong emotions in healthy ways, such as using relaxation and breathing exercises, singing or listening to music, exercising and taking care of our body, journaling or writing laments, and talking with others.

C. By thinking through our responses to difficult decisions in advance

F | *(1 min) Present content below.*

During crises we often face difficult decisions. If we consider these situations in advance and decide how we want to respond, we are more likely to act in a way that is consistent with our beliefs.

DISCUSSION

F | *(5 min) Small group. Assign one of these scenarios to each group. Mention that there is not always a clear answer to these questions, but it can help to think through our response before a crisis.*

Choose one of the situations below. Read all or some of the Scriptures and discuss the questions.

F | *(18 min) Large group. Get feedback. Add content below each set of questions that was not mentioned.*

1. What if you only have enough food for your family, and your neighbors come and ask for food? Read Luke 10:30–37, 1 Kings 17:9–16, and 1 Timothy 5:8. Then discuss the questions that follow.
   - According to Luke 10, who is your neighbor?
   - In 1 Kings 17, what happened to the widow's flour and oil when she shared it with Elijah?
   - In 1 Timothy 5, who does Paul say you should care for especially?
   - Are there times you should say no to your neighbors? Explain.

It is good to share, but if everyone has been told to prepare in advance, those who have prepared are not necessarily obliged to help those who have neglected to do so. Pray about each situation that arises and ask God for wisdom.

2. What if an angry person threatens to kill you if you don't allow them to steal things from you? Read Matthew 6:24–33, Hebrews 10:34, and Luke 12:15. Then discuss the questions that follow.

- In the Matthew passage, what does Jesus teach about possessions?
- How did the people in the Hebrews passage respond when their possessions were seized?
- What might lead us to hold on to our possessions so tightly?

People whom God has made matter much more than material goods. Goods can be replaced later on; people cannot. We should be willing to give up our possessions rather than be killed.

3. What if there is civil unrest and people have broken into a supermarket. A friend says, "Let's take some food!" Your family is hungry. How should you respond? Read Exodus 20:15, Romans 13:1–5 and 8–10, and Matthew 6:25–34 and 7:7–11. Then discuss the questions that follow.
   - In Exodus 20:15, what are we commanded not to do?
   - What reasons are given in Romans 13 for obeying the laws of the land?
   - What can Matthew 6 help us realize when we are in need?
   - What does Matthew 7 tell us to do when we are in need?

In the chaos after a disaster, people may think no one will notice if they loot, but God sees. If everyone starts looting, chaos increases, causing more suffering.

4. What if there is a natural disaster in your area, and your church is asked to be a shelter for displaced people, even though the church members have very few resources themselves? Read Proverbs 24:3–6, Ephesians 5:15–17, Philippians 2:4, 1 John 3:17, and Matthew 25:35–40. Then discuss the questions that follow.
   - In the Proverbs passage, what are the most important parts of a careful plan?
   - The Ephesians passage contrasts wise and foolish people. What makes the difference?
   - According to the Philippians passage, what should we care about?
   - According to the passages in 1 John and Matthew, how does God view our service (or lack of service) to people in need?

We should be willing to help others in need. However, we must also be wise in how we act. There may be special safety requirements for a shelter. If your church is unable to provide housing, perhaps there are other needs that the church can meet for displaced people like assistance with food or clothing. Those trained in helping others emotionally and spiritually could provide support for those who are struggling.

5. What if an enemy tells you to kill someone or he will kill you? Read Revelation 21:1–7 and Exodus 20:13. Then discuss the questions that follow.
   - What will happen to Christians when they die?
   - What does God say about murder?

The Bible tells us that God has good plans for his people in the age to come. If a Christian is killed, that is not the worst thing that can happen. A person is made in the image of God. To kill someone is very wrong in God's sight. Sometimes God intervenes and the enemy does not carry out the threat.

6. What if an enemy says you must denounce Christ in order to stay alive? Read Mark 8:31–9:1, Acts 4:13–21, and Revelation 3:7–10. Then discuss the questions that follow.
   - In the Mark passage, what does Jesus say his followers must do?
   - What does Jesus say about someone who tries to hold on to his own life rather than following Jesus?
   - In the Acts passage, why do Peter and John refuse to obey the religious leaders?
   - In the Revelation passage, why does Jesus praise the church of Philadelphia?

It is never right to deny that we follow Christ, but sometimes this can be very difficult. If we deny Christ, we will feel great shame and guilt. We can remember the story of Peter, who denied Jesus three times, yet Jesus restored him (John 13:37–38; John 18:17, 25–27; John 21:15–19).

7. What if you are hiding people from an ethnic group that is being killed and their enemies come to your house? If they ask where these people are, how will you answer? Read Joshua 2:1–16. Then discuss the questions that follow.
   - Why did the spies come to Jericho? Who sent them?
   - Why did Rahab lie to the officials of Jericho?
   - Was she right to lie? Why or why not?

There may be cases where it is right to deceive those who are seeking to do evil. This needs careful discussion because it is wrong to tell lies under normal circumstances.

Closing   5 min

DISCUSSION, IN PAIRS

F | *(4 min) Pairs.*

1. Write down at least one thing you can do in each of the following areas to prepare for a future disaster or crisis, then share with another person:
   - Practical preparation
   - Communication plan
   - Spiritual preparation
2. What is one thing you want to remember from this lesson?

F | *(1 min) Close the lesson by praying for the participants and the community. Consider practicing a breathing or relaxation exercise with participants, since talking about future troubles can make people anxious.*

Preparing to lead your own healing groups

Welcome to the global community of tens of thousands of people who have walked a healing journey using *Healing the Wounds of Trauma*. Many have become facilitators who are able to lead other people through the same healing journey.

Here are the steps to becoming a trauma healing facilitator:

- Experience at least the core lessons of *Healing the Wounds of Trauma* as a participant
- Get an overview of the trauma healing program
- Learn the essentials of facilitating groups
- Demonstrate the ability to facilitate a group in a participatory way (through a practice facilitation exercise)
- Demonstrate understanding of the content of the lessons (through a test)
- Learn how to organize a healing group and to access the materials one needs to do so
- Plan two healing groups you intend to lead

A global community growing

F

Trauma healing program overview

Trauma Healing Institute

Trauma Healing Institute (THI) is a global organization dedicated to helping people around the world heal from the pain of trauma. We support individuals, churches, and other organizations with ministry tools and resources they can use to help people heal in their own communities.

THI method

At the heart of the THI method is a book called *Healing the Wounds of Trauma*, which contains a set of practical lessons that lead people on a journey of healing. At the heart of the book is the Bible, which tells us about the love of God. The book and supporting materials are available in over 150 languages, and new translations are being added all the time. (See page 208 for the history of *Healing the Wounds of Trauma.)*

The THI method brings a group of people together in a safe place where they can help each other heal. This **healing group** is led by facilitators who have been trained to help people who are in pain, without hurting them more. In the healing group, people learn how to talk about their own pain and listen to the pain of others. They find comfort for their hearts and minds in God, who cares for all of us, and in a community that walks the road of healing with them.

A healing group

There are **five characteristics** that make this method uniquely effective.
1. It brings together proven mental health practices and the wisdom of the Bible in a way that is accessible to everyone.
2. It is designed for anyone to use, with simple language and clear ideas that are easy to understand.
3. It happens in small groups, led by trained facilitators who do not need to be professional counselors.
4. It uses a participatory format to help people engage deeply with themselves, with God, and with each other.
5. It is adaptable, so people can use it anywhere in the world, in any language or culture.

THI program model

The THI program model usually uses the following stages:

- **Convening session:** to help leaders experience and understand the trauma healing program and decide if they want to integrate it into their ministry.
- **Equipping session:** to train people to lead healing groups. This is done through a three-step process: an initial equipping, a practicum (leading two healing groups), and an advanced equipping to finish the basic training. Some participants are selected to help lead trainings.
- **Healing group:** to help people with heart wounds find healing, engage with Scripture, and become more resilient. They meet in a small group (ideally 6–12 people) and cover at least the six core lessons.
- **Trauma healing mini-session:** to address trauma related to a specific need, but without covering the six core lessons. It is often one lesson or portions of several lessons.
- **Community of practice:** the network of facilitators using these materials. At times they gather for networking, collaboration, professional development, encouragement, and prayer. They may invite mental health professionals and leaders from organizations and churches that work with trauma survivors.

THI materials

Trauma healing materials are available for different audiences and purposes, and more programs are in regular development.

- *Healing the Wounds of Trauma: How the Church Can Help.* Participant book for healing groups. The original trauma healing program for adults (often referred to as the "classic" program). Also available:
  - *Scripture Companion Booklet.* For participants in a healing group who do not have a Bible or are not accustomed to looking up Bible verses, or for new readers who find a booklet easier to read than a Bible. Contains the main ideas of each lesson and Scripture passages written out in full.
  - *Facilitator Guide for Healing Groups.* For participants at an initial training who will be leading healing groups. Contains instructions and timetables for each lesson and practical guidance on leading a healing group.
  - *Advanced Facilitator Handbook.* For participants at an advanced trauma healing training. Contains additional material about leading healing groups and caring well for traumatized people, along with guidance in leading trainings and other trauma healing events.
- Correctional editions. *Healing the Wounded Heart: Participant Journal.* An adaptation of the core lessons of *Healing the Wounds of Trauma* for use in correctional facilities. Complemented by the *Facilitator's Guide for Inmate Journal* and the *Advanced Facilitator's Guide.*
- *Healing Hearts Club Story and Activity Book* and *Healing Children's Wounds of Trauma: Facilitator Book.* The Bible-based trauma healing program for children ages 8–13. The ideas in *Healing the Wounds of Trauma,* communicated by means of stories, games, exercises, crafts, and activities.

F

- *Life Hurts, Love Heals: Teen Journal* and *Healing Teens' Wounds of Trauma: Facilitator's Guide.* This version of trauma healing is recommended for use with teens and young adults ages 14–20, depending on the culture. It follows an urban-based story that addresses identity, family traumas, grief and loss, types of traumas young adults tend to face, and more.

- *Story-based Trauma Healing.* For use by live storytellers. Presents the same ideas as *Healing the Wounds of Trauma,* but communicated orally by means of Bible stories, current life stories, exercises, and memory verses put to song. Literacy is not required for facilitators or healing group members. Recordings of the stories and exercise instructions are available, as well as a Story Book with discussion guide and a facilitator handbook.

- *Audio Trauma Healing.* Professionally produced audio dramas of current life stories and Bible stories, with small group discussions and Scripture songs. For broadcasting by radio or other devices. Available in mp3 format. May be used in training and listening groups where literacy is not required for listening group leaders or members. Discussion guide for leading listening groups available.

For more information about these materials and about being trained to use them, visit traumahealinginstitute.org or contact your local Bible society.

Becoming a trauma healing facilitator

Facilitator competencies and capacities

1. Able to manage personal well-being
2. Able to work on a team
3. Able to help traumatized people
4. Able to lead groups in a participatory way
5. Demonstrates understanding of the content
6. Committed to leading healing groups

See the appendix for details.

Training process
TRAINING PHASE

Step 1: Initial equipping

Purpose:
1. Explore own heart wounds
2. Learn to help others

Outcome: Participant may be certified as **Apprentice Facilitator** and authorized to do a practicum.

Step 2: Practicum

Purpose:
1. Gain experience using HWT material and participatory method
2. Help healing group participants find healing

Outcome: Participant is eligible to attend advanced equipping.

Step 3: Advanced equipping

Purpose:
1. Discuss successes and challenges of the practicum
2. Strengthen facilitation skills
3. Learn to care better for self and others
4. Plan for trauma healing ministry phase

Outcome: Participant may be certified as **Healing Group Facilitator** and possibly a **Training Facilitator**.

MINISTRY PHASE

Outcome: Hurting people find healing in healing groups.

Supporting outcome: The number of healing groups increases as Training Facilitators lead convening sessions and equipping sessions.

See "Facilitator gifts, callings, and activities" in the appendix for details.

Facilitating groups

Facilitating groups well requires three things: participatory learning, using visual aids well, and managing group dynamics.

A. Participatory learning

DISCUSSION

1. Think about how we have been doing this trauma healing session and compare it with other seminars or classes where you heard people lecture, or sermons where you heard someone preach. How has this session been different?
2. What are some of the different ways you have participated in this session?

In a traditional teaching method, the focus is on the teacher lecturing or delivering information. In the participatory method used in this program, the focus is on the learner engaging with the material. Rather than simply receiving information, the learner participates in the learning process. The goal is for the learner to understand, apply, and be changed by it.

This trauma healing program allows people to participate through group discussions, art expression and lament exercises, role plays, exercises to practice new skills, and self-reflection.

DISCUSSION

What might be some benefits of using a participatory method, compared to a traditional teaching method?

Benefits of the participatory method

- Participatory learning respects the knowledge and experience the group brings. The facilitator first learns what people in the group already know, instead of wasting their time by trying to teach what they already know. **Don't tell people what they already know; do tell them what they don't know.**
- It allows people to interact personally with the ideas so they understand how they might benefit from them.
- It allows for engaging the mind, emotions, and body all together, which makes for the best learning experience. We remember those experiences in which our emotions are stirred and our bodies are involved far more than those which only engage our thoughts.
- It involves humor and creativity. Laughter helps people learn. Creativity involves other parts of the brain, leading to greater learning. The more creative, the better—and people can be surprisingly creative.

DISCUSSION

What does a facilitator need to do to make the participatory method effective?

To make the participatory method effective:

- Be aware of how engaged the group is and adjust your approach to keep the energy flowing.
- **Give up some control** as the leader and take risks because you can't predict what people will say. The risks are well worth it!
- **Be flexible.** If people ask questions about something you plan to cover later in the lesson, discuss the topic then, if possible. People will remember it better! Throw the question back to the group ("What do you all think?") and get their input first, as this will give you time to organize your thoughts and add anything not already stated. Adjust the timing of the rest of the content you were planning to cover.
- **Have a plan for off-topic questions.** People can ask questions that are good but are not related to the topic of the lesson. Designate a flip chart paper or part of the board as a "refrigerator" or "parking lot" where these questions can be stored for a later time. Be sure to find a time to respond to these!
- **Create a safe space.** Invite people to share but don't pressure them. Avoid shaming them by disagreeing with them publicly. Discuss confidentiality (page 191). Use name tent cards or name tags and provide other ways for people to get to know each other and begin to trust one another.
- **Ask–Listen–Add.**
  - ◆ **Ask:** Say just enough to introduce the topic and ask the discussion questions (or give instructions for an exercise). The questions in the book have been carefully crafted and tested around the world. You can trust them. If needed, you can distribute the questions among the small groups.

    Your goal in asking the questions is to have participants interact with each other and answer each other's questions, rather than relying on you for the answers. Imagine that you toss a ball (the question) to them and then they toss the ball among themselves.
  - ◆ **Listen:** If participants are discussing the question or doing the activity as a large group, listen in order to learn what they already know. If they are divided into small groups or pairs, get feedback in the large group afterward. If they ask you a question during the feedback time, it is most effective to toss the question back to the whole group, since someone else may know the answer.
  - ◆ **Add:** If participants did not mention all the important points from that section of the book, ask if anyone has anything else to add before adding it yourself. You do not need to say everything in the section. Then transition to the next section of the lesson.

F

- **Follow the "5-minute rule."** Do not talk more than five minutes without participation from the group. Avoid repeating things that the participants already said. When you talk, it should be to encourage participation, thank people for what they said, add new information, and briefly summarize and transition to the next topic.
- **Prioritize participation, especially working through their emotions and practicing the new skills.** The participants' participation is the most important part of the learning process, as they talk about their pain and do the listening exercise, the art expression exercise, the lament, and the other activities.
- **Be realistic about how much you can do in the time allotted.** Guide the group without giving the impression that you don't have enough time. There is no need to say things like, "We're short on time so we'll skip that." Keep the session participatory and skip some content if necessary. It is helpful to think through in advance which verses or sections you will skip if time runs out. At the end of each lesson, encourage the participants to read the lesson and look up the Scripture passages after the session. Be sensitive to the needs of your participants: whether they are flexible to stay longer, or if they need to leave at the ending time that was announced.

DISCUSSION

Why might the participatory method be helpful for people recovering from trauma?

The participatory method and trauma:
- Trauma silences people's voices because it seems too horrific to put into words and it disrupts the normal way our brains put words to events. A participatory approach gives people the opportunity to recover their voice, as they tell their stories to each other.
- Trauma disconnects people from others. A participatory approach reconnects people in ways that contribute to their healing.
- Trauma affects the entire body. A participatory approach includes mind, emotions, and body, all of which are necessary for healing.

B. Using visual aids well

DISCUSSION

What types of objects or visual aids have we used, during this session, to illustrate ideas or help people remember what has been said?

In this program we use things like flip charts/whiteboards, diagrams, and props (like water bottles in a tub of water) to help people remember what has been said.

When writing on flip charts/whiteboards:
- Only write the important things. If you write everything, what's important will no longer stand out. It also gets monotonous. It is better to write less.

- Write clearly and large enough so people can read it. People don't benefit if they can't tell what is written.
- Stand to one side of what you're writing so people can see it.
- The discussion is the main activity. The writing should support the discussion, not steal the focus.
- Consider having someone else scribe for you. This allows you as the facilitator to stay engaged with the participants and to maintain eye contact with them. Allow time for the scribe to write before moving on.

The use of computer-driven presentations using PowerPoint is discouraged because they can keep you from responding to the unique dynamics of the group.

C. Managing group dynamics

The following table offers a list of challenges that can arise in a group, along with ideas on how to deal with them.

Challenging behaviors	Possible solutions
Talker: This person dominates groups by talking all the time.	"Let's hear from someone else now." It can also be helpful to review the group's commitment to sharing the time and giving everyone a chance to speak. Consider asking participants to limit themselves to one or two comments per discussion. Sometimes people like this are not aware that they are dominating, and you may need to talk to them privately.
Quiet: This person says nothing at all.	"What do you think about this question?" Don't force a quiet person to share if they don't want to, but do try to make space for them to do so if they wish.
Off-topic: This person can take any subject off course, in a different direction than the facilitator wishes.	Respectfully remind them of the topic and guide the group back to the question currently being discussed. Use the "refrigerator" as necessary (see page 181).
Misinformed: This person gives wrong information.	Ask the group if anyone else would like to comment. Let the group correct itself, if possible, but do not let wrong ideas go uncorrected. Remember to always be respectful.
Overwhelmed: This person erupts in sobbing and tears, unable to contain emotions.	Find someone who can go with the person to a quiet place where they can talk.
Overwhelming: Someone may tell their story in such a graphic way it traumatizes others.	Before sharing begins, orient people to share their stories but not dwell on horrific parts as this may be upsetting to others.

F

Challenging behaviors	Possible solutions
Spiritual fixers: No matter the problem, this person is quick to offer a Bible verse and advice. They minimize the pain of others or try to fix everyone rather than listen.	Before the sharing begins, make it clear that the group is there to listen, not to fix or solve problems.
Offensive: Someone may be culturally inappropriate or disrespectful of other faith traditions.	Ensure that no one is marginalized. You may need to challenge someone privately for the good of the group.

Practice facilitation exercise

Instructions

The practice facilitation exercise allows you to get experience facilitating in a safe environment and with feedback from others. You will role play a small healing group (4–6 people), with each of you taking turns as the facilitator. The others will act like this is their first time discussing this content (this is not the time to enact the "problem behaviors" described above!).

There are two typical kinds of challenges in practice facilitation:

1. People who have worked as teachers or pastors are used to talking, not listening. It can be a challenge to shift the way you do things and let the participants do more talking than you do. To help yourself, sit down in a chair in the circle when you facilitate, instead of standing. Imagine that you are holding a microphone when you are talking. Your goal should be to give the microphone to the participants the majority of the time, since healing is more likely to happen when they are talking, not when you are talking.

2. People who are not used to being in front of groups can get stage fright. The best way to get over this is by practice. To help yourself, focus on asking the questions and listening well while you let others talk. Be gentle with yourself, as you would be with a toddler learning to walk or a child learning a new skill.

You will be the facilitator for only **ten minutes**. The main points to remember in your ten minutes are:

1. In your brief **introduction**, assume that the group has discussed all the preceding lesson material up to this point. You can explain how your topic is connected to the preceding topic; you can be creative; or just follow the facilitator manual.

2. Then **ask** the discussion question. Limit your introduction and asking the question to 2 minutes.

3. **Listen** as the group discusses the question for 6 minutes. Or break the group into pairs for 3 minutes of discussion, followed by 3 minutes of sharing their responses in the whole small group.

4. After the discussion, you should **add** any important points that were not covered. If everything was covered, make a summary of the main points that were expressed. This should take about 2 minutes.

5. The timekeeper will hold up a 5-minute card when you are halfway through, then a 2-minute card, and then a finish card.

Preparation

In small groups, select one of the discussion questions from the lessons you covered (excluding "Bringing our pain to the cross"). Each person in your group should select a different question. Do not select the stories at the beginnings of the lessons. The following questions work well:

- What does your culture tell you God is like, especially in times of suffering? (Suffering lesson, Section 3A, question 1)

- What do the following verses teach us about God in times of suffering? (Suffering lesson, Section 3A, question 2; choose one or two verses)
- Think of a deep cut on your arm: How does it heal? What helps it heal? Now let's compare a physical wound to a heart wound. (Heart wounds lesson, Section 2A, discuss some, but not all, of the comparisons)
- With what kind of person would you feel free to share your deep pain? (Healing lesson, Section 2B, after the skits)
- When you have been grieving the loss of someone or something, what sort of helpful things have people done or said? What sort of unhelpful things have been done or said? (Grieving lesson, Section 5, question 1)
- What do the following verses say about why we should forgive? (Forgiveness lesson, Section 4; choose one or two verses)

Use the template below to prepare.

Step		Minutes
Introduce What will I say to introduce the topic?		
Ask What is (are) the discussion question(s)? Will we discuss in pairs or as a whole small group?		
Listen As they discuss, I will listen. If they discuss in pairs, I will get feedback afterward.		
Add What are the main points I will add from the book, if they are not mentioned? What will I say to conclude?		
What materials and visual aids do I need?		Total =10 minutes

Feedback and evaluation

At the end of each practice facilitation exercise, you will respond to two questions:

1. What do you think went well?
2. What would you do differently next time?

Then each group member will give you feedback using the same questions.

Your facilitating skills will be assessed on a scale from 1–10, with 10 as excellent.

- *Very Good* (9–10 points): Communicates material from the book very clearly and accurately. Group participation organized very well. Responds very well to questions. Keeps the group functioning well. An enjoyable learning experience.

- *Good* (7–8 points): Communicates material from the book clearly and accurately. Group participation organized well. Responds well to questions. Some small issues in managing the group.

- *Fair* (5–6 points): Communicates material from the book accurately. Some group participation. Presentation or group participation not always well-planned or clear. Has some difficulty responding to questions and managing the group.

- *Weak* (3–4 points): Either preaches or lectures with very little or no group participation, or the presentation is confusing or inaccurate or focuses on material not in the book. Does not respond satisfactorily to questions. Not able to manage the group.

- *Very Weak* (1–2 points): Unable to communicate in a group. Unable to manage a group.

F

Organizing a healing group

See the healing group checklist in the appendix for a list of the facilitator responsibilities described below. See the THI facilitator website for recommendations for leading an online healing group.

Before starting the group

A. Getting authorization

Before you begin your healing group ministry, you need to get authorization from the appropriate leaders. The program overview brochures at the Trauma Healing Institute website may be helpful as you explain the program.

Healing groups are part of a local ministry and should not require external funding, except possibly for the materials. In many cases, participants or local sources can cover the cost of at least the Scripture Companion Booklet.

B. Forming the group

Facilitators:

- It is ideal for facilitators to work in teams of two, so they can balance each other's strengths and weaknesses and support one another.
- If there is no other facilitator who lives near you and with whom you can lead:
    - stay in close contact with your mentor as you prepare your group and as you lead it.
    - choose a friend who is gifted in caring for people to help you, and go through the lesson with him or her first.

Participants:

- The ideal number of participants in a healing group varies, but 6–12 works well. If the group is larger than this, it will be helpful to break into smaller table discussion groups so that everyone has an opportunity to participate. Each small group should have a facilitator.
- A group should be made up of people who are able to discuss the topics together comfortably. This varies according to the culture, but if women cannot speak in the presence of men, or youth in the presence of elders, organize separate healing groups.
- People do not necessarily need to share the same kind of trauma to form a healing group. The effects of trauma and paths of healing are similar regardless of the source of the trauma.
- Participants can be personally invited to a healing group, or it can be announced publicly. A flier template that can be customized to announce a healing group is available on the facilitator's section of Trauma Healing Institute website.
- If a potential participant has very recently experienced trauma or has very high trauma symptoms, have a conversation with them beforehand to determine if the healing group is the right fit for them, in terms of timing and content.

- It is recommended that no new participants be allowed to join the healing group after it begins and that visitors not be allowed, unless everyone in the group is in agreement that they may join.
- Trust and continuity of the lessons are important parts of experiencing the full healing process. It is important that participants start with the group and come to all sessions. If someone has to miss a session, they should tell facilitators in advance, when possible. Another person can go over materials with them before the next meeting.

C. Scheduling the group

A healing group needs to cover at least the six core lessons. You can meet for several days in a row, like a retreat, or in once-a-week meetings spread out over several months. The total amount of time needed to cover the Welcome session, core lessons, and the Looking back session is 12 hours (see Time required for each lesson, in the appendix).

Processing too much pain and trauma too quickly can harm participants rather than help them. If we push people to feel too many emotions too quickly, the healing group can be as traumatic as their original experience. Therefore, **do not cover more than three lessons in a day. Never try to do all the lessons in one day.**

Lesson order

In addition to the core lessons (in bold below), you can include the optional lessons (in italics) in the order indicated below, according to the needs of your group and the time you have available. In some contexts, it is better to wait to do the Suffering lesson until after you have done the Heart wounds, Healing, and Grieving lessons.

If God loves us, why do we suffer?
What is a wound of the heart?
  Moral injury
What can help our heart wounds heal?
What happens when someone is grieving?
  How can we help children who have experienced bad things?
  Rape and other forms of sexual assault
  Recovering from abortion (downloadable)
  HIV and AIDS
  Domestic abuse
  Suicide
  Addictions
  Caring for the caregiver
Bringing our pain to the cross
How can we forgive others?
  How can we live as Christians in the midst of conflict?
  Preparing for trouble
  Helping people immediately after a disaster (downloadable)

Do "Bringing our pain to the cross" after completing the first four core lessons and as many of the optional lessons as you have chosen, so that participants have had an opportunity to reflect on the pain in their hearts. Do "How can we forgive others" after "Pain to the cross" because it is much easier for people to forgive those who have hurt them once their pain has begun to heal.

D. Preparing the lessons

Study each lesson as you prepare to facilitate it. Pay attention to the following:

- **Sections**: Divide the sections of each lesson between you and your co-facilitator. When working together for the first time with a co-facilitator, assign the lessons for the first sessions but wait to assign the rest until you get to know each other and learn who is best at what.
- **Timing**: The timetable at the beginning of each lesson can help you plan your use of time. It also allows you to see the lesson structure at a glance. The lessons are designed for sessions of 90–120 minutes (see Time required for each lesson, in the appendix). If you have more time, adjust to your situation. If you have less time, discuss with your mentor how you can modify them. Some exercises, like the art expression exercise and the lament exercise, can be explained in the group meeting, given as homework, and then discussed the following meeting.
- **Stories**: Each lesson starts with a story that depicts the problem the lesson addresses. These stories should be presented aloud and discussed. The purpose of the stories is to get the participants thinking about the subject and sharing their ideas. Present the story in one of the following ways:
  1. Tell the story in an engaging way.
  2. Divide the story into sections and have different participants read different sections.
  3. Have someone read the narration parts and give the dialogue parts to different individuals who will read at the appropriate time in the story.
  4. Have the participants act out the story (with either gestures or words) as someone reads it.
  5. As someone reads the story section by section, have participants draw a picture expressing either the action or emotion represented in the section. (Give time in between the sections for them to draw.) Read the story a second time, as participants review their drawings. This process takes more time, so use it only when time limits are not a problem.
- **Adjusting the stories**: The stories refer to imaginary people and places. If you adjust them, be sure not to use real places, names, or ethnic groups, as this can support stereotypes and cause conflicts. If it would be helpful in your context to feature female lead characters in the story, or characters from a different Christian tradition, adapt the stories accordingly.
- **Scripture references:** Review the Scripture references in the lesson, including those in parentheses. You may find that some of the extra verses are helpful during the discussions or to answer questions. Remember that it is not necessary to use all the verses during the session. If your group is not familiar with the Bible, you should plan to explain some of the background for the verses listed for discussion.

- **Discussions**: If your healing group is very small, feel free to do all discussions together rather than dividing into "small group" and "large group" discussions. If you have at least four people, consider dividing into pairs occasionally. If you have a healing group of six to eight participants, break into small groups of two or three from time to time.
- **Materials**: If possible in your context, provide each participant with a copy of either *Healing the Wounds of Trauma* or the Scripture Companion Booklet. For situations where one of more participants are not fluent in the language of your book, seek to include multilingual people among the facilitators or participants, to translate.
  1. Singing together can be helpful at a trauma healing session. If group members do not know the same songs, provide a song sheet so everyone can sing together. A sample song sheet is downloadable from the THI facilitator's website.
  2. Paper, markers, and pens are needed for the Word Art activity, the art expression exercise, and writing laments. A flip chart is often helpful. Have facial tissue available.
  3. A cross and matches are needed for the "Bringing your pain to the cross" exercise. A rope (or something else that can be used to tie two people together) is needed for the lesson on forgiveness.
  4. Certificates of participation are appreciated in some contexts. See sample in the appendix.

E. Preparing to care well for your participants

Local resources

Before you start your group, identify any local counselors or agencies that could help participants who need more care (domestic abuse, sexual assault, addictions, suicide, and so on).

Confidentiality

The process of trauma healing requires a safe space for people to work through the materials and their own experiences. As a condition of their participation, members of healing groups are asked not to share information about others in the group. We can tell our own stories to anyone we wish, but we can only tell someone else's story with their permission. The Bible repeatedly warns against gossip and indicates that a trustworthy person keeps a secret.

The facilitator will also maintain confidentiality. There are certain situations, however, where it may be necessary for a facilitator to share information with others. Consider the situations below and research in advance the laws in your country.

1. **Abuse of a child**. If, during the course of a healing group, a facilitator learns that a minor is being sexually or physically abused, he or she must report it immediately to the proper authorities (police, child abuse hotline) and later to the church or ministry leaders, if appropriate. In many places failing to report can result in legal consequences. Reporting requirements vary, so it is important for facilitators to learn the requirements in their area. (In the U.S., see childwelfare.gov for information on federal and state guidelines).

   The motivation for reporting is not simply to avoid legal consequences. The protection of those who are vulnerable, especially children, is at the heart of the Christian faith (Matthew 18:6; Proverbs 31:8; Psalm 82:3–4; Deuteronomy 24:17; James 1:27). Christians are to speak up for those who are being abused and to seek justice, not just do the legal minimum. Reporting abuse against children is always the best thing for the church and for victims, even if it seems to hurt more at first. If your church or ministry does not already have abuse prevention and reporting procedures, seek local expert help to craft such procedures.

2. **Abuse of elders and people with disabilities**. While reporting this kind of abuse to authorities is not required by law in all countries, it is encouraged.

3. **Abuse of an adult**. Facilitators are not required by law to report physical or sexual violence against an adult, and doing so could harm the victim. Reporting must never be done without the victim's permission and should never be forced. Such decisions should be for the purpose of safety and include the victim in the planning whenever possible.

4. **Suicide**. Facilitators and people who are not mental health professionals are not required by law to report suicidal people. However, they should consider safety measures (see Suicide lesson) and calling the police.

5. **Homicide**. If a facilitator learns of a participant's intent to harm another person, the facilitator is at liberty to warn the intended victim and should strongly consider notifying the police.

During the group

A. Arranging the space

The group can meet in a home or a room at a church. Participants should be seated in a way that allows them to interact with each other in a circle or around a table. The group can agree on whether refreshments should be served and if so, how to do it.

B. Managing the time

Start and stop the sessions at the times agreed upon. If some participants want to continue the discussion beyond the session time, close the meeting to allow people to leave. Then those who choose to stay can continue.

At the beginning of each meeting:

- welcome participants as everyone arrives and allow a few minutes for people to connect,
- then begin with a brief devotional or prayer,
- review the group commitments/guidelines, and
- briefly review what was covered at the last meeting and let participants know what to expect in the current meeting.

An important part of the healing process is for participants to share the trauma they have experienced. There are many opportunities for this throughout the lessons. Prioritize this sharing time over your speaking time, as this is the most important part of the healing process. Participants should share without accusing others or giving so many details that they upset others.

The Word of God gives life and feeds people's souls. Take time to look up the Scripture references that are in the lessons and read them aloud.

If you are giving the participants their own copies of *Healing the Wounds of Trauma,* have them close their books after the story is read at the beginning of each lesson. The book has all the content the facilitators will be sharing, so they do not need to take notes unless they want to. Encourage them to read the lesson and look up the references after the session.

C. Wrapping up the group

Be sure to finish the final session in an appropriate way. Here are some ideas.

- Consider doing the "Looking back and looking forward" section and as many of its closing activities as appropriate. Discuss whether the group would like to continue with other material.
- Share contact information among group members, if they would like to do so. In areas where security is a concern, it may be better to form a social media group using an application like WhatsApp and ask participants if they would like to join.
- Be sure to get permission for photos. Use the individual and/or group authorization form as needed (see appendix).
- Some participants appreciate receiving a certificate of completion at the end of the healing group. See the appendix for a sample.
- Give participants the opportunity to fill out the participant feedback form. See the appendix for a sample.

After the group

A. Debriefing with your co-facilitator

Meet with your co-facilitator and discuss the following questions:

- What were the successes?
- What were the challenges?
- What will you do differently next time?
- Will any of the participants need follow up?

Review the participant feedback forms.

Sometimes after people have participated in a healing group, they decide they would like to become facilitators. They can do this in three ways:

1. attend an initial equipping session, or
2. attend a Becoming a Facilitator session that reviews the *Healing the Wounds of Trauma* lessons and covers all the lessons in this "Preparing to lead your own healing group" section, including the practice facilitation exercise and the test, or
3. have a certified Training Facilitator lead them through a review of the *Healing the Wounds of Trauma* lessons and all the lessons in this "Preparing to lead your own healing group" section, including the practice facilitation exercise and the test.

B. Reporting your healing group

After your healing group, you and your co-facilitator will fill out a healing group report (only one report per healing group). Send it to your mentor or your trauma healing coordinator. See the sample report in the appendix.

DISCUSSION

What are some reasons that reports may be helpful?

These reports are vital to the work of trauma healing because they:

1. help facilitators reflect on what they have done well and what might need to be done differently next time. They also document the good things that happened and serve as a source of encouragement.
2. tell THI which facilitators are active in which locations. This is especially important when THI receives requests from people needing trauma healing.
3. encourage financial partners, ensuring that the program can reach more traumatized people, and inform and expand the local community of practice.

C. Gathering testimonies

If a participant has experienced healing through the healing group, writing and sharing their testimony can be a further step in their healing journey. Testimonies can bring glory to God and can also encourage people who are supporting your ministry.

If you would like to share people's testimonies with others, ask them if they are willing to have their story shared. Never pressure them. If they're willing to share, have them sign the individual authorization form (see appendix). If you write the story for them, let them review the story before you share it with others and withdraw authorization if they wish. Their well-being is the first concern.

A testimony should include three parts:

1. the person and the problem (give details)
2. the trauma healing input that took place (give details)
3. how the person changed (give details)

Also be sure to get permission for photos. Use the individual and/or group authorization form as needed (see appendix).

Leading a trauma healing mini-session

At times you will have an opportunity to present one or more of the *Healing the Wounds of Trauma* lessons to address a specific need, instead of covering all six core lessons. This is called a **trauma healing mini-session**.

To lead a mini-session, you will need to create a safe environment for sharing, by including at least the following:

- Doing a welcome session, including a discussion of how to make the group safe for everyone (Welcome, Section 2)
- Defining what is a wound of the heart and comparing a heart wound and physical wound (Heart wounds lesson, Section 2A)
- Discussing how people with wounded hearts behave (Heart wounds lesson, Section 2B)
- What is a good listener like, including the three listening questions (Healing lesson, Section 2B)
- Listening exercise (Healing lesson, end of Section 2)
- The grief journey (Grief lesson, Section 3)

Talk with your mentor before you lead your mini-session to learn if there is anything else you should include, given the unique opportunity before you.

When the session is complete, fill out and submit a mini-session report form (see appendix).

THI website

At traumahealinginstitute.org, you can access information on Trauma Healing worldwide, including upcoming events and trainings, videos, brochures in English, French, and Spanish, and more.

You can also create an account which will allow you to access materials to help in promoting, leading, and reporting your healing groups. To create an account:

- click "Log in" (upper right)
- click "Sign up"
- agree to the terms and conditions and click "Sign up"
- verify your account through the message sent to the email address you provide
- return to the website and log in.

Once your trainer enters your certification level, you will gain access to the "Materials" page (upper left of your Profile page).

F

Action planning

The next step in your training is to complete two practice healing groups, ideally within the next six months. These two healing groups qualify you for the advanced equipping. (The more time that passes without using this material, the less you will remember and the less confident you will be. An Apprentice Facilitator certification expires after 24 months of inactivity.)

Use the following questions to guide you in planning your two healing groups. Work in pairs with someone you expect to be your co-facilitator. Work individually if you are in an isolated location.

☐ Step 1. What leaders do we need to meet with to present the program and get their support before we start?

☐ Step 2. Who are the people in our location who could benefit from a healing group? How many are there? What is the maximum number of participants we will have in our group?

☐ Step 3. How would we inform our potential participants about the group?

☐ Step 4. Where would be a convenient, comfortable location to hold meetings?

☐ Step 5: Which lessons do these people need besides the core lessons? How many sessions will we need to complete all the lessons?

☐ Step 6. On what dates and days, and at what times will we and our potential participants likely be available to meet?

☐ Step 7: What materials will we give them? (*Healing the Wounds of Trauma,* Scripture Companion Booklet, etc.)

My mentor's name:_____

Email:_____

Phone:_____

I will complete two healing groups so I can take the advanced equipping session in _____ (date). Here is my plan:

    I will notify my mentor when I am about to start each healing group.

    After each healing group, I will submit my healing group report to_____

APPENDIX

Facilitator competencies and capacities

1. Able to manage personal well-being.
• Demonstrates emotional stability. Not overwhelmed with personal or family issues.
• Demonstrates good self-care.
• Demonstrates ability to set appropriate boundaries with participants.
• Responds to the stress of facilitation in healthy ways.
• Helps others without being overwhelmed.
2. Able to work on a team.
• Gives and receives constructive feedback.
• Dependable to carry out assigned tasks.
• Addresses conflict in a timely and gracious way.
• Relates well to those of different church traditions/cultures/races/gender.
• Demonstrates awareness of his/her impact on others.
3. Able to help traumatized people.
• Shows concern for confidentiality.
• Listens well and validates participants' experiences.
• Develops trust and shows genuine care for others.
• Allows people to process and share their feelings.
• Responds appropriately to the emotional climate of the group.
4. Able to lead groups in a participatory way.
• Emphasizes participants' knowledge and contributions. Avoids preaching and lecturing.
• Able to present in an engaging way.
• Manages participant feedback and problem behaviors well.
• Manages time well.
• Able to judge which sections to lengthen/shorten/omit depending on context and audience.
5. Demonstrates understanding of the content.
• Shows satisfactory grasp of key ideas of the program.
• Facilitates in accordance with the objectives of lessons and sections.
• Able to transition well between sections of a lesson.
6. Committed to giving time to trauma healing.

A

Facilitator gifts, callings, and activities

Discerning if you are apt to become a facilitator and the kind of facilitator that matches your gifts and calling is done prayerfully over time in dialogue between you, your trainers, and your organizational leaders.

Certification means that THI agrees that you have the competencies necessary to carry out a trauma healing ministry. These competencies can improve over time, and your mentor may work with you to develop a plan for continued learning.

If ever it becomes apparent that you are lacking in a competency, your certification may be put on 'inactive' status while you take time to improve in that area. This is both for your benefit and the benefit of those you minister to.

Certification level	Gifts and callings	Activities
Healing Group Facilitator (*the most important role in the program*)	• interpersonal relationships • discipleship • **helping individuals** in small group settings	Help wounded people by: • leading healing groups • listening to and supporting individuals using the HWT principles
Training Facilitator	Same as above, plus: • equipping others for ministry • organizing and leading training events • speaking to large groups	Continue to lead healing groups, and equip others to become effective Healing Group Facilitators by: • organizing and helping facilitate initial equipping sessions • approving and mentoring new Apprentice Facilitators • being mentored by a more experienced facilitator
Master Facilitator	Same as above, plus: • strategizing and managing ministry programs • spotting problems and finding solutions	Continue the above activities, plus promote the growth of trauma healing programming by: • organizing and helping facilitate advanced equipping sessions • approving and mentoring Training Facilitators • strategizing and taking action to promote trauma healing ministry • participating in the further development of the program

Time required for each healing group lesson

CORE LESSONS	TIME
Welcome	20 min
If God loves us, why do we suffer?	2 hours
What is a wound of the heart?	1 hour 30 min
What can help our heart wounds heal?	2 hours
What happens when someone is grieving?	2 hours – 2 hours 15 min
Bringing our pain to the cross	1 hour 30 min
How can we forgive others?	2 hours
Looking back & looking forward	30 min
Total (minimum)	12 hours

OPTIONAL LESSONS	TIME
Moral injury	2 hours
How can we help children who have experienced bad things?	1 hour 30 – 40 min
Rape and other forms of sexual assault	1 hour 50 min
HIV and AIDS	1 hour 45 min
Domestic abuse	1 hour 50 min
Suicide	1 hour 35 – 40 min
Addictions	2 hours – 2 hours 10 min
Caring for the caregiver	1 hour 30 min – 45 min
How can we live as Christians in the midst of conflict?	1 hour 45 min – 2 hours 10 min
Preparing for trouble	1 hour 45 min

A

Healing group checklist

See the THI facilitator website for the most current version of the checklist.

BEFORE

- ☐ Get authorization from appropriate leaders to hold a healing group.
- ☐ Find facilitator to co-lead healing group.
- ☐ Determine venue of healing group. Identify a location based on local needs, cost, and accessibility for attendees.
- ☐ Determine dates and schedule of healing group.
  - Include at least the welcome session, six core lessons, and "Looking back."
  - Be sure to debrief the art and lament exercises if participants do them as homework.
  - Do not schedule more than three lessons in one day, to protect participants from becoming overwhelmed emotionally.
  - Schedule snack/meal times, if applicable.
  - Get input from your mentor about your intended schedule.
- ☐ Calculate costs. Healing groups are a part of a local ministry and should not require external funding. The only costs should be for materials, books, food, and beverages.
- ☐ Divide lesson sections with the co-facilitator.
- ☐ Study and prepare for lesson sections. Practice skits and exercises, prepare Bible references, music (if applicable).
- ☐ Purchase/prepare materials.
  - *Healing the Wounds of Trauma* participant book or Scripture Companion Booklet (one for each participant)
  - Tissues
  - Bibles, if needed
  - Pens/pencils
  - Name tags or name tent cards
  - Markers/crayons
  - Blank paper
  - Flip chart, flip chart markers and/or whiteboard and markers
  - Song sheets
  - Cross, if permissible
- ☐ Prepare to care well for participants. Research local resources to which you can refer participants, if needed, and laws regarding confidentiality.
- ☐ Monitor registration list. Often, some people who register are not able to come, so keep a list of additional people who would like to attend. Remember that once the group begins, new participants should not be added, unless everyone in the group agrees.
- ☐ Arrange for interpretation for participants, if needed.
- ☐ Oversee the provision of food, drinks, and snacks, if applicable. It is helpful to have a host who is responsible for this so you can focus on the lessons.

☐ Remind participants of group details, such as:
- Dates and start and end times
- Schedule
- Importance of attending all sessions. Participants should speak directly with the facilitator about scheduling conflicts.

☐ Meet with co-facilitator(s). Talk through the schedule. Ensure all sections in each lessons are covered and that you have all the needed materials. Pray for the participants, the staff, and the session.

☐ Set up meeting space. Arrange tables and chairs in a way that allows participants to interact, ideally in a circle or at table(s). Try to make it a pleasant environment.

DURING

☐ Meet with co-facilitator at the end of every session. Discuss learnings from session, participant concerns, and schedule modifications for the next session. If needed, talk with your mentor about any concerns.

☐ Touch base with participants regularly. Find out how they are feeling and if they are having any difficulties as a result of the healing group experience.

☐ Connect with your mentor at least once during the healing group, to talk through any questions.

☐ Print participation certificates, if appropriate.
- Some contexts appreciate certificates, while others do not care as much. Determine if certificates would be helpful.
- Download the healing group participation certificate from the THI website. Fill in location, date, and each participant's name. Print and sign.

☐ If photographs are taken, ensure that participants sign the group authorization form.

☐ If testimonies are given, ensure that participants sign the individual authorization form.

☐ If desired, give participants the opportunity to fill out the participant feedback form.

AFTER

☐ Debrief with co-facilitator. Review participant feedback forms.

☐ Send your healing group report form to your mentor or TH coordinator.

Sample healing group participation certificate

Download this file from the THI facilitator website.

Healing group report

For the most current version of this report, see the THI facilitator website.

Country:	Main facilitator:
City:	Assistant facilitator(s):
State:	Main language:
Did you meet online? ____ Yes ____ No	Host organization:
Begin date: / End date:	Implementing partner:

Count of hours: _____	Duration: ☐ weekly ☐ twice/week ☐ half days ☐ all day ☐ other	Local funding? ☐	Confidential? ☐ *(Check only if security risk)*

Audience (optional):	☐ First responders ☐ Non-Christians ☐ Foster parents ☐ Orphans ☐ Incarcerated ☐ Pastors ☐ Military people ☐ Refugees ☐ Missionaries ☐ Students ☐ Muslims ☐ Trafficked people	# who started: ____ # who completed: ____	# who are: ____ Male ____ Female
		# who completed who are: ____ Anglican ____ Catholic ____ Protestant ____ Orthodox ____ Other: _____	

Materials: ☐ Audio ☐ Classic (Adult) ☐ Military ☐ Generational Trauma ☐ Correctional ☐ Story-based	**Lessons:** *Core* ☐ Suffering ☐ Heart wounds ☐ Listening ☐ Lamenting (for Audio, SBTH) ☐ Grief ☐ Pain to the cross ☐ Forgiveness *Supplemental or program specific* ☐ Children ☐ Rape ☐ HIV and AIDS ☐ Domestic abuse ☐ Suicide ☐ Addictions ☐ Caregiver ☐ Christians living amidst conflict ☐ Preparing for trouble ☐ Helping after disaster ☐ Covid-19 ☐ Moral injury ☐ Abortion ☐ Generational trauma (Gen Trauma) ☐ Community grief (Gen Trauma) ☐ Other: _____	What successes did you experience? What challenges did you face?

Please provide two testimonies, with photos and authorization.
Send the report to your mentor or TH coordinator.

Trauma Healing Institute

Group authorization for photographs and recordings

Copy this page or prepare a sheet of paper with the text below and ask participants to print and sign their name to authorize use of photos and recordings that include them. Send this authorization form, with the photograph or recording, to your mentor or trauma healing coordinator.

Date:_____City, state, country:_____

Facilitator(s):_____

I authorize the Trauma Healing Institute and their partners to use photos and/or voice/video recordings that include me, to promote their trauma healing programs. I am 18 years old or older.

Name	Signature

Trauma Healing Institute

Individual authorization for testimonies, photographs, and recordings

If a testimony, photo, or recording can be traced to an individual, get permission before sharing. Use this form or create your own with this wording. Send this authorization form, with the testimony, photograph or recording, to your mentor or trauma healing coordinator.

Description of the item: _____

I authorize the Trauma Healing Institute and their partners to use the materials in question in their ministry of promoting trauma healing programs. The material in question is mine and I willingly give this authorization.

Name:_____ ☐ I am 18 years old or older.

Signature:_____ ☐ Do not use my name.

Date:_____City, state, country:_____

Facilitator(s):_____

Trauma Healing Institute

Participant feedback form

Name (optional):

☐ *Check this box to grant permission to use your comments anonymously for trauma healing advocacy.*

1. Which session did you find most helpful? Why?

2. Which session was most difficult for you?

3. Are there things you expected to learn at this session that were not covered?

4. What changes, if any, do you think could improve the healing group?

5. How has this healing group impacted you (for example: learning something new, your own healing, feeling better able to help others, etc.)?

6. Do you have any other comments?

Trauma Healing Institute

Trauma healing mini-session report

Name: _____ For the month of: _____

Date				
Location				
Kind of group				
1st contact? 2nd? 3rd?				
Contact hours				
Main facilitator(s)				
Assistant facilitator(s)				
Lessons or parts of lessons/ exercises done				
Language(s) used				
Number of participants				

Attach testimonies and photos, with authorization. Send report to your mentor or TH coordinator.

Trauma Healing
Institute

A

History of *Healing the Wounds of Trauma*

If people have had terrible things happen to them, can God heal them? Can the Bible help? These are questions that the authors of this book were each asking in the late 1990s as they saw people suffering as a result of war. At the time, there was very little to help church leaders in rural areas find answers to these problems. Margaret Hill (SIL Africa Area Scripture Use Coordinator), Richard Baggé, and Pat Miersma (SIL Africa Area Counseling Ministries) found one book that was helpful: *Healing the Wounds of Ethnic Conflict: The Role of the Church in Healing, Forgiveness, and Reconciliation* by Rhiannon Lloyd. Using this book as a model and with Lloyd's agreement, they decided to write a different type of book for local church leaders. It would be easy to teach, easy to translate, and easy for church leaders to teach to others. In addition, it would incorporate best mental health practices. Margaret developed and piloted four lessons in Democratic Republic of the Congo, with the help of Ngbaka church leaders, then worked with Richard and Pat to develop drafts of more lessons.

In 2001, Margaret, Richard, Pat, and Harriet Hill (SIL Africa Area Anthropology Coordinator) met with the following group to further develop the materials: Anzelekyeho Abiti (Bible translator); Londroma Bandony (pastor, DRC); Karl Dortzback (Institute for the Study of African Realities); Joyce Fiodembo (counselor); Emmy Gichinga (counselor); Edward Kajivora (ACROSS and Sudan Literature Crusade); Pio Lokoro (Bible translator); Violette Nyrarukundo (counselor); Anastasse Sabamungu (African Evangelist Enterprise). The lessons were tested in war zones and were first published in 2004 by Paulines Publications in Nairobi. By 2011, people in forty-two countries on five continents were using the book and it had been translated, in whole or in part, into 157 languages.

More and more people asked for training in trauma healing at the same time that American Bible Society (ABS) became interested in trauma healing. So in 2011, the authors gave ABS permission to provide the needed infrastructure to expand the reach of the program, and ABS made Harriet Hill their Trauma Healing Program Director. She coordinated the development of materials and the program model for *Healing the Wounds of Trauma*, for example, story-based, audio, and video trauma healing, an on-line database for reporting and a website. ABS convened the Trauma Healing Advisory Council, comprised of mental health professionals, to be sure that the best mental health principles were used. The Nida Institute at ABS helped ensure that Scripture was being used correctly.

In 2012, ABS established the Trauma Healing Institute to support and develop the program. That same year, Harriet initiated the first "Community of Practice" gathering to bring together organizations and individuals working in the area of trauma healing. The Community of Practice became a part of the program model, at international, national, and local levels. In 2016, Harriet initiated the Trauma Healing Alliance to provide multi-agency leadership to the further development of the program. Major revisions of *Healing the Wounds of Trauma* were released in 2013 and 2016. This 2020 revision continues with the most recent developments of the materials and model.

Throughout all these developments, the basic approach the authors used from the start has been maintained:

- Trauma healing is based on what the Bible and mental health experts say.
- We adapt the book and program to fit the local situation.
- We try materials out with participants in various settings and revise them until they work well.
- We train local people to teach the material.
- We work mainly with groups rather than individuals.
- We use participatory learning, because people learn best this way and it helps them to heal from their trauma.
- We work in ways that let churches and communities continue trauma healing on their own.
- We encourage organizations to work together to help the many people suffering from trauma.

Acknowledgements

We thank all those who have contributed to make this book what it is. First, we recognize the Christians in Africa whose suffering compelled the authors to look at Scripture with fresh eyes and be engaged with it.

We acknowledge the seminal work by Rhiannon Lloyd in *Healing the Wounds of Ethnic Conflict: The Role of the Church in Healing, Forgiveness, and Reconciliation* (Mercy Ministries International) that emerged from the aftermath of the 1994 Rwandan genocide.

Healing the Wounds of Trauma has evolved thanks to the many church leaders who have used these materials and have provided insight and feedback on how to communicate effectively to those suffering from trauma. We thank them for their passion and companionship.

We thank SIL International and Wycliffe Bible Translators, who encouraged the authors to respond to the trauma needs of the people they had grown to love, and who supported their efforts to do so.

We thank the many people who have helped in the development of these materials. We specifically acknowledge the contributing authors of the lessons added in later years: Carol King, Harriet Hill (ABS), and Phil Monroe (ABS) for Domestic Abuse, Suicide, and Addictions; Pat Miersma (SIL) and Stacey Conard (SIM) for Moral Injury. We are deeply grateful to hundreds of other trauma healing facilitators from all over the world who gave input into this new edition.

We thank the many volunteers who have taught, translated, and lived out the principles in these materials so people and communities broken by trauma can be restored to wellbeing.

We thank the many mental health professionals who have contributed their expertise to the development of these materials. We especially thank the members of the Trauma Healing Advisory Council, along with the many donors who have enabled this ministry, especially Mrs. Swannie te Velde, who funded the first publication of the book in 2004.

A

We are particularly grateful for the partnership of the Canadian Bible Society, George Pabi, and Tomas Ortiz in producing this 2020 revision of the book and supporting materials. Their pioneering spirit and expertise in Paratext have laid the foundation for faster, more accurate translations of trauma healing materials in the future.

Most of all, we bring our thanks and praise to Jesus Christ, who took all the suffering of the whole world upon himself on the cross, and whose wounds bring us healing (1 Peter 2:24).

About the authors

Margaret Hill received her master's degree from the University of Manchester, UK, and has worked with SIL International since 1968 in Bible translation and Scripture Engagement. Richard Baggé, MD, a psychiatrist with SIL International since 1993, studied medicine at Jefferson Medical College and Duke University Medical School. Pat Miersma received her Master's in Nursing in ethnic mental health at UCLA and has served with SIL International counseling since 1980. Harriet Hill received her Ph.D. in Intercultural Studies from Fuller Seminary, worked with SIL for 32 years, and worked with the Trauma Healing Institute at American Bible Society for ten years.